Paige, Daniel,
May Farrah & Demi
grow to be resilient
and courageous!

Bruce Kidd Bramble
Santa Barbara
Sept - 2021

Book Two in the Lumberjack Jesus Series

Raising God's Gen Z Teen

33 Strategies to Teach Teenagers Self-Reliance, Confidence & Responsibility

Bruce Kirkpatrick

Print ISBN: 978-1-7330410-5-8
Ebook ISBN: 978-1-7330410-4-1

Praise for
Raising God's Gen Z Teen

Far too often, we get caught up in the breathless pace of life and find ourselves parenting by circumstance and chance. In today's culture, with our Gen Z kids, we need to have a strategy with purpose and meaning. In this excellent book, Bruce has given parents a practical blueprint for raising our teens to thrive. All 33 strategies combine for a wonderfully relevant look at raising your kids to become responsible adults who make good choices.

—Jim Burns, Ph.D.
President, HomeWord
Author of *Understanding Your Teen* and *Doing Life with Your Adult Children: Keep Your Mouth Shut and the Welcome Mat Out*

Few things are as important as parenting teenagers. Bruce has lived out the wisdom of this book. His practical insights, deep soulfulness and godly wisdom comes through and will be well underlined and earmarked by every parent that picks it up. A great tool for any parent navigating the choppy waters of raising teenagers!

—Dr. Jon Ireland
Lead Pastor, Oceanhills Covenant Church

Engaged parenting at its best. In *Raising God's Gen Z Teen*, Bruce Kirkpatrick offers an accessible, action-oriented resource for effective parenting fueled by a vision for the future. The strategies shared direct parents' energies to the modeling, discussion, and connection that equip teens to bring their gifts to the world. Throughout the book, there is a pervasive emphasis on loving relationships as the path to parental influence. Infused with biblical principles, this book is a valuable addition to every parent's toolbox.

—Leanne Leak

Former Early Education Field Director, Western States, ACSI; co-author of *Attentive and Attuned: Knowing and Serving in the Early Education Program*

This book is a must-read for all parents! The world our teens are trying to navigate today has never been experienced before! Written in an easy flowing format, each chapter stands on its own and is followed by discussion questions. It is humorous and enjoyable to read. I would have given anything to have had this tool when my children were teens.

—Jeneane Stevens, MEd

Executive Director, Celebration Center

In *Raising God's Gen Z Teen*, Bruce Kirkpatrick offers guidance for parents and caregivers facing the challenges of raising adolescents in the 21st century. With a dose of practicality and a sprinkling of humor, this book is easy to read and filled with examples and activities you will find helpful as you guide your teen on the journey to establishing life goals. Through this process, your child will be prepared to face situations that may test their faith, but to which they will make good choices.

—Dr. Constance M. Youngblood

Instructor of Educational Leadership and Middle and Secondary Education, Edinboro University of Pennsylvania

Thirty-three times, Bruce "hits the nail on the head" with wisdom and insight into what matters most when raising a teenager during these unpredictable times. A must-read for parents of teenagers today.

—Ed Wimberly, Ph.D.

Author of *Parenting with an Attitude: Twenty-One Questions Successful Parents Ask Themselves* and *How They Make It Work: 21 Habits of a Successful Marriage*

Dedication

For my children and my grandchildren—and for
my grandchildren not yet born.

Also by Bruce Kirkpatrick

Fiction

Hard Left

The Resurrection of Johnny Roe

The Carnival Chemist and Other Stories

Non-Fiction

Lumberjack Jesus: How to Develop Faith Despite Pitfalls, Roadblocks, Stupidity, and Prejudice

Acknowledgments

There are way, way too many people to thank for their participation in this book. So many friends shared their stories and ideas with me as I kept digging deeper into these strategies. Nuances, tips, and details emerged, and even though my name appears as the author, we all had a part in it.

My editor, Virginia McCullough, helped craft inconsistent ramblings into something I believe could help shape a generation. Her expertise from 30,000 feet and deep into the weeds of the manuscript are unique, insightful, and kind and warm-hearted. Except for those details where I seemed to use a hatchet instead of a keyboard. Then, she was relentless. And I cherish her for it.

A special thanks to Connie Youngblood for her support and encouragement. I still have a class photo of first grade at North End School in Meadville, Pennsylvania, where Connie was a classmate. Never underestimate the benefits of a lifelong friendship.

I could not have survived raising children without the calm, loving, and enthusiastic partnership of my wife, Nancy. She's always the best part of us.

As always, thank you, Jesus.

Table of Contents

Preface

In writing *Lumberjack Jesus: How to Develop Faith Despite Pitfalls, Roadblocks, Stupidity, and Prejudice,* I discovered a God I didn't always see in the Bible. A God that is loving, a good conversationalist, and often looks like a lumberjack. I found that as anger, shame, and guilt consumed me from an early age—quite literally dying on the inside—Jesus came to me looking like a lumberjack, in a red plaid shirt and a short-cropped beard. (It emerged from an image I'd seen in William Paul Young's book, *The Shack.*) Even as I became confused about "religion" or I pushed Jesus so far away and with such belligerence that reconciliation seemed impossible, Jesus was always around and available.

He became my source of insight, wisdom, compassion, and grace. My foundation, my rock. Through the haze and confusion of what it means to fully accept Christ as both a savior and a friend, I constructed a visual guide in that book to develop an honest, practical faith. It's chock-full of scripture, prayers, and anecdotal examples.

The book you are reading now is the second in the Lumberjack Jesus series. I've used many of the same Biblical principles—and Jesus as the guiding light—to build strategies to raise responsible, resilient, and self-confident teens who grow into adults not only with purpose, passion, and self-esteem but as people with an extra dose of God's wisdom, compassion, and grace.

Introduction

Every time my wife pushed during the delivery of our first child, the heart rate monitor plunged, indicating the umbilical cord was wrapped around the baby's neck, choking him. The doctor simply reached in, grabbed the cord, and pulled it over his head, releasing it back inside my wife. As I look back, that was a harbinger of life with our son. Panic. Wonder. Wow.

We felt like successful parents if we could keep that little boy fed, bathed, and occupied for a long enough stretch of time that one of us could get some shuteye. *Okay,* we thought, *we can figure this out.*

But it's never that easy, is it? As our son grew and new situations popped up, we immediately felt the deep, uncharted, and murky waters or raising children.

After our second child was born and they both turned preschool age, my wife found a school that was close to home, clean, and friendly. It happened to be Christian. We quickly recognized not only the care and attitude of the staff rubbing off on our kids, but they also taught great lessons in how to treat people, raise children, and become dependent on God's message. Even at an early age we could see the benefit for our kids—a self-confidence to deal with life, not get too stressed, and to show love.

My wife Nancy and I had been raised in Christian households—in the 1950s and '60s, Christianity was foundational to everyday life in the United States. Our families didn't read the Bible daily and attended church only sporadically, but the Ten Commandments still adorned public buildings, schools still practiced prayer, and The Golden Rule exemplified the way we treated each other.

Today that influence is much diminished. We live in a post-Christian era in America—Christianity has lost much of its influence over society. Only 22 percent of men and 28 percent of women attend church on a regular basis.

I'm not a youth pastor or clinical psychologist. But I've worked with kids as a father, coach, mentor, and businessman for over forty years, and I see a fundamental change in child-rearing in the U.S. today. Many parents have shifted away from a Christian foundation and adopted a child-centric approach.

We see this shift away from Christian values in society in general—a little darker, uncaring, less optimistic, more self-centered. Maybe we only recognize it now because of the 24/7 news cycle and the proliferation of snarky social media.

Building and boosting children's self-esteem as the primary goal of child-rearing became vogue a generation or more ago. I would never advocate against self-esteem because I know the benefit, but over-emphasis can produce lopsided children, concerned first with themselves and relegating others— including their parents at times—to a second-class position.

The Bible never advocates putting yourself first. It always emphasizes loving God and your friends and neighbors above loving yourself.

Can we discover a path to self-reliance and responsibility for today's teenagers through a model of care, forgiveness, exploration, and joy? I believe so. And I know it can lead to fulfilling lives of meaning, purpose, and passion—what most kids, and adults for that matter, strive for. In this book, I use strategies from the Bible, and especially Proverbs, to illustrate these points of emphasis. Although I only touch on some of the much tougher topics facing today's teens—sexual conduct, bullying, suicide, and mental illness—my strategies can influence all aspects of your children's lives.

We can take self-centered, lopsided children and help form them into adults that exude self-reliance, confidence, and responsibility. We can stop being helicopter parents, hovering over our little ones, protecting them from this big, bad world. We can help them develop a "life plan" that positions them for success and fulfillment.

If we only see the Bible as a set of rules—do this, don't do that—then we miss the love and grace and freedom that Christ offers. Similarly, if kids see parenting as a restrictive book of what they can and cannot do, then they miss the love and support you want to convey to them as parents. Let's find a balance of boundaries for their benefit matched with a guide to help them explore and grow into the adults we all want them to be.

America desperately needs young adults cultivated and nourished to be self-reliant, confident, and responsible. The American teen—much maligned these days for their dedication only to their cell phones and local tattoo artist—is nonetheless positioned remarkably well to succeed in life. This next generation, Gen Z (born in the late 1990s through the early 2010s), can have a life better than ours or our parents. It's certainly possible—no matter what the preponderance of pundits says about America heading downhill.

As with any generation, this vision starts with parents. Parents willing to change their own habits—from cell phone use to sweating the small stuff—to set the example for these impressionable kids.

Next to those first couple years in a baby's life, the teen years may be the most crucial time for parents. You'll be bombarded with hormonal explosion, huge jumps in developmental growth—both physically and emotionally—and relationships so fundamental and critical to a teen's success. A teenager needs parental instruction, support, and empathy now more than ever.

This book about raising teens evolved from many different sources. I scoured not just the material that's been written for parents, but other books about:

- Success
- Goal setting
- Teamwork
- Leadership
- Making an impact
- Caring for others
- Finding passion in life
- Humor

The strategies in this book will teach teens:

- To experience self-worth without conceit
- To feel loved without guilt and shame
- To find humor in life without ridicule
- To seek passion in career and pursue it
- To develop a vision for their successful future
- And yes, to communicate without using their phones

They also teach parents the same things.

Our job as parents is to teach, to explore, and to expose our teens to as much of life as we can while we still have influence with them. To prepare them to face the challenges that life will inevitably throw their way. To help them thrive. To grow up self-reliant, confident, and responsible. To use their God-given gifts and talents to make an impact, to seek fulfillment and joy.

Are you well equipped to send them on that journey, parents?

You possess a great privilege and a huge responsibility. You'll need to set the example and the standard for your child. You'll need to be resilient and responsible yourself. As you grow into that role as a parent—as we all do—your child will flourish. You may, too. Your American Gen Z teen will be well equipped to meet today's world head-on. To thrive when others falter. To succeed when others suffer. To grow to be the adults who shape our future for the better.

#1

Express Your Love

Did I offer peace today? Did I bring a smile to someone's face? Did I say words of healing? Did I let go of my anger and resentment? Did I forgive? Did I love? These are the real questions. I must trust that the little bit of love that I sow now will bear many fruits, here in this world and the life to come.

—Henri Nouwen

D id your parents say they loved you? Out loud? I don't remember mine expressing love that way more than occasionally. They showed it all the time, but they didn't say it much at all. Maybe just my family or their generation didn't verbalize love well. Let's make sure *this* generation hears it more.

We all want to feel loved. It's one of the most basic human needs. Right up there with air, water, and food. Most children know, deep down, that their parents love them. But they also want to hear it, continually. Knowing that they are loved boosts their outlook, elevates their mood, and instills them with pride and self-esteem.

You may never have actually heard God speak words of love to you—in an audible way. (Or maybe you have, halleluiah!) But you've read about the many ways Christ expressed his love throughout the Bible. That's pretty much the main theme of the whole book: love.

Find ways to express your love verbally to your child—and don't quit when they become teenagers. Around the age of ten, some boys may turn away when you try to hug them or not acknowledge when you say you love them. But it doesn't mean they don't want to hear it.

Girls at that age typically still like hugs, but as they approach the teen years, it suddenly may become "uncool" to receive affection from Mom or Dad in front of their peers. Parents go from cool to lame pretty quickly for some kids.

But don't let that stop you.

The best way to express love? Verbalize it. Please don't tell me you're not the kind of person to say those things out loud. That doesn't quite cut it with kids—or wives or husbands either for that matter. If you haven't learned to express your love verbally...all I can say is learn how to do it, now, please. I realize there are other "love languages" that we use to express love, including spending quality time and physical touch. This is not a book about learning how to verbalize your emotions, but if you don't do that well, maybe it's time to practice. Work together with your spouse, practice on your dog or cat...whatever it takes, learn to verbalize your love.

Have heart-to-heart discussions with teens. Tell them how much you love them, especially after they make mistakes or are feeling down about something. Tell them that nothing they do will ever negate that love. Convey to them that you will love them no matter what. Don't hold your love back until they fulfill some prerequisite. No "I'll love you if..." language. If you get good grades. If you love me back. If you do your chores. Or if you fulfill some promise you made. Don't even *infer* this type of trade—exchanging your love for something in return. Because if you don't receive that something, then you'll continue to hold back that love.

After you verbalize it, document it. Write them a card, a note, or a letter with your love expressed. Something they can keep and cherish and refer to when it seems like you *don't* love them. We've all read stories of dog-eared notes of love, affection, or encouragement hidden in wallets or purses for decades. Kids keep these love notes because they make a profound impact on their lives.

Don't simply document it once. Send little notes or cards regularly and especially during those times when they're vulnerable and need to hear it—and see it.

Make those love declarations a common occurrence and a unique treat. Tell them you love them consistently, every day. Make those more regular love announcements a practice. Do it frequently, either as a typical greeting each time you see them or a farewell when they leave the home. For example, each morning as they leave for school.

Tell them at special times, too, when they aren't feeling loved—when they are down, depressed, or defeated. Make it a point to pull them aside and one-on-one express your confidence in them and your unrelenting love. This is for their ears only—from your lips directly to their heart.

Don't get trapped into expressing love with presents or gifts. A new phone, a new outfit, even a new car. Here's an extreme example. In the high school my daughter attended, graduation presents for a very select few of the girls included...wait for it...breast augmentation. Seriously. The boys got new cars, and the girls got new... looks. Can you believe that?

If your family is affluent and you have the means to give

your children cars or other gifts, I'd like to recommend a great book. *The Price of Privilege* by Madeline Levine, Ph.D. The subtitle says it all: *How parental pressure and material advantage are creating a generation of disconnected and unhappy kids.* In the book, this clinical psychologist explodes various child-rearing myths and identifies parenting practices that are toxic to healthy self-development and contribute to an epidemic of depression, anxiety, and substance abuse.

Do not teach children, especially teenagers, that objects like presents or gifts are a substitute for love. It never works; they'll come to expect material things and not genuine affection. Teach them to expect the verbal expression of love, a sincerity from the heart and not the pocketbook.

Don't overdo the gifts—overdo the love.

When your child matured from birth into adolescence, you may have expressed your love in mostly tactile ways, like cuddling and hugging. Once children understand verbal language, the best way to teach them your love is by saying it. Out loud, often, and from the heart.

When children feel loved, it's a natural self-esteem boost. You won't have to find many other ways to instill value in a child other than giving them undeniable, unrelenting love.

Parenting Tip

Some evening, without warning or agenda, visit your teen in their room. Sit and chew the fat, whatever fat comes up. Start with some open-ended questions, like:

- How was your day?
- What're you working on?
- How's life treating you these days?

Offer advice if you have any, but don't make that a priority. Lend an ear because you have two. Taking time to listen is often more powerful than offering advice. Then end the one-on-one time with your child with a simple, "I love you." You can preface it with phrases like, "however it turns out" or "whatever you decide" or "regardless of what happens"—I love you. They don't have to say it in return. You just need to say it so *they* hear it.

Parents Prayer

Dear heavenly Father, teach me how to express love to my kids in every way that I can. Help me tap into your unlimited supply of love, especially when I'm not feeling it. Give me encouragement to never hold back my love for any reason. Make me an example of your unconditional love to my whole family. And others, too. Thank you, sweet Jesus. Amen.

Stretch the Strategy

1. Discuss with your spouse how love was expressed in your respective households growing up.
2. Discuss with your friends, Bible study groups, and extended family how love was expressed in *their* families.
3. Develop with your spouse a list of acceptable ways to express love in your immediate family. To begin, make them verbal and non-gift expressions. Then expand as you see how initial ideas work.

#2
Teach Your Teens to Listen for the Voice of God

What we do with our love will become the conversations we have with God.

—Bob Goff

Whatever your vision of a higher power—God, Abba, Father, Mohammed, Yahweh, Jehovah, Jesus, King of Kings, El-Shaddai—comfort emerges in knowing that there is a power in control. When *you* try to manage all aspects of your life and the life of your teen, disappointment can mount because it often seems like an impossible task. If your teen cannot or will not listen to you about the Most High, then teach them the characteristics of a benevolent being, a good God.

1. *God is good.* God does not bring evil into the world. Evil exists, but it has nothing to do with God.
2. *God responds to His people.* God protects all of the people who cry out. He provides for them.
3. *God knows every detail of your life.* Nothing is beyond or out of reach for God. He sees all and knows all.

4.   *God allows free choice.* The choice to follow God is yours. He never forces his will upon you.

5.   *God has a plan for each person.* He is in control. He has a plan for your life.

6.   *God loves His people.* God created the Earth for the sole purpose of providing a place to love his people and for them to love others. God is love.

If you can believe that "God is love," you can listen for the voice of God by looking for love in all the right places. God never deceives. God never lies. God never confuses. That's the devil working, not God.

So, how would you teach your teen to live their life as if they were listening to the voice of God? Glad you asked because I have a few ideas.

1.   *Do good.* If God is good and you have the choice of doing good or not, then do good.

2.   *Do what is right.* If God never does evil and you are faced with a right vs. wrong question, do the right thing. I know it's not always easy to pinpoint, but many times it is. Even when it hurts, we can do right. Even when we have to sacrifice something, we can do the right thing.

3.   *Do to others what you'd want for yourself.* This is the Golden Rule, revised a bit. If God is all about protecting and providing for people, and you see a chance to protect, provide, or give to another, go do it. That's following God's voice.

4.   *Do what is fair or just.* God gives favor but also provides justice. If you are questioning some situation in life, wondering what to do, by simply doing what is fair or just —equal parts good for you and good for the other person—that's what God would do. In other words, don't take advantage, don't try for the upper hand, don't "I win, you lose"; go for the win-win.

The good-good.

5. *Love one another.* This is the ever-elusive, ever-present goal of life. It is not "he who accumulates the most, wins in the end" philosophy. That's marketing hype. It is not "win at all costs"; that's an "us vs. them" personal warfare. It's love your fellow man. It starts with the family. Teach your teen to love their mom and dad and their brothers and sisters. Teach them what love means. Then teach them to love their friends, teachers, neighbors, and everyone they meet. Notice I didn't say everyone who's good to them. Everyone! No exceptions. That means heeding the voice of God. It's no easy task and you, parents, may need to clean up your own life before preaching this one to the kids.

You didn't suspect this would get so mushy? You don't know how to teach your children to love? You'll see this theme—loving each other—throughout this book. Like these:

- *#1: Express Your Love.* Tell your child that you love them. Express your love in words!

- *#2: Teach Your Teens to Listen for the Voice of God.* He loves you, provides for you, knows you, and has a plan for you. Listen.

- *#6: Teach Your Teens to Accept Apologies and to Forgive.* Let it go, move on, don't hold a grudge. Forgive, forgive, forgive. I can't say it enough.

- *#8: Teach Your Teens to Contribute to Others.* It's not all about you.

- *#12: Teach Your Teens to Thank Others.* A simple but effective sign of love.

- *#16: Help Your Teens Keep Their Promises.* Don't go back on your word; don't let people down. Love them.

- *#23: Help Your Teens Explore and Discover Their Passions in Life.* About life, about loving, about others.

That's enough for now. You can always go through the list of strategies and hear the voice of God in almost every instruction I will convey to you.

I know it's not always easy to listen and sometimes it's even harder to hear God's voice. But start somewhere. Begin today. Find the time—make the time—to listen. The earlier you guide your children to hone in on the voice of God, the more impact your voice may have on their lives. God will support you, parents. And then your kids begin to develop their own voice, enhanced by God's influence. Living solo and trying to figure things out all alone is a very difficult way to go through life. It's lonely, it's barren, it's discouraging, and it leads nowhere.

Don't know God? Go find him. Read a Bible. Visit a church. Ask your friends. You'd be surprised how many among you know and listen to God every day. He's not hard to find, and He's always available. Ask around.

Parenting Tip

The voice of God is not always a voice. I believe I've actually heard God speak to me, in words, twice in my life. But he speaks to me in other ways. Through a verse in the Bible. From a book someone else has written. In a dream or a vision (an awake dream.) In the voice of a loved one or friend.

You can ask your child as they try to decipher if something is coming from God:

"Does that sound like God to you?"

Now your child may have to research what God wants for

us, but that's a good thing, too. In my book *Lumberjack Jesus: How to Develop Faith Despite Pitfalls, Roadblocks, Stupidity, and Prejudice*, I recap a few truths about God:

God is good.

He wants you to be joyful.

You have nothing to fear from God.

God brings good, not evil.

His grace is sufficient.

Love wins.

God wins.

Does that sound like God to you? It does to me.

Parents Prayer

Most High God, I know that you are good. That you want me to be joyful and full of love. I believe I have nothing to fear from you. I know that in this life, your grace is sufficient for me—it's enough, it's all I'll ever need. I know that love wins. I know that in the end, you win, Lord. Hallelujah! Thank you, sweet Jesus. Amen.

Stretch the Strategy

1. What spiritual practices do you use to help you hear the voice of God?

2. Describe a time when you knew what you were hearing was God communicating. How did it happen? What did you learn from that experience?

3. If you're having trouble hearing God, ask your pastor or small group how they decipher God's voice.

#3

Pray and Teach Your Kids How to Pray

But when you pray, go into your room, close the door and pray to your Father, who is unseen. Then your Father, who sees what is done in secret, will reward you.

—Matthew 6:6

Praying is a wireless connection to God—Bluetooth, no data charges. Like telling a good friend your problems, praying allows you to get things off your chest. But unlike your good friend, God can do something about your problems or requests. I know, that's hard to believe, isn't it? You get the picture of Jim Carrey in the movie *Bruce Almighty* at the keyboard, and he's getting millions of prayer requests every second. He's overwhelmed—they just keep coming. Finally, he does a "select all" and says YES to every one of them. I love that scene.

I don't know how he does it, but God reacts to every prayer as if it was the only thing on his mind in the world at that moment. He's not only a good God, but a personal one, too.

I understand that if you were not raised with prayer—and many Christian families aren't—it can seem intimidating or mundane or downright ridiculous. And if you don't really know whether you believe in God, prayer can seem a waste of time. But I will give you over thirty ways to teach your children how to be self-reliant, confident, and responsible, so perhaps you will indulge me on this one. Give it a try; what could it hurt? If prayer is between you and God—and I know that often prayer happens in groups—but if you begin with just the two of you, nobody will know that you're praying. If it doesn't work, you've only lost a little time. If it does, you've gained the best coach and mover-shaker in the universe. Small price to pay, wouldn't you say?

Here's a great way to learn how to pray.

1. *Start simple.* Begin to pray simple prayers. That's what God prefers anyway. Parents, you could start praying for a release of anxiety toward your teen. Maybe repeat that small prayer numerous times a day for several days or weeks. Notice if you are less anxious. If you are, prayer answered! If not, don't give up the prayer. God may be telling you that your anxiety is well warranted.

2. *Pray what you are feeling.* If you can expand your prayers, simply tell God what you're feeling. If not anxious, then proud, sad, overwrought, worried, hassled, clueless—you name it. Whatever you can express, God can understand.

3. *Pray "thank you."* Just like how we teach our children to thank others, God likes to hear it, too. Pray thanks for whatever you want for your children—a sunny day, a good disposition, a good grade on a test, no arguments, clean fingernails, no missed curfews, well-directed enthusiasm, being on time, a kiss on the cheek. The side benefit: you begin to notice and appreciate the good things in your children's lives, not just the negative. You become the cheerleader, not just the critic. I guarantee your child will notice the change in you.

4. *It's okay to ask.* The Bible says God hears our requests and answers. Now, you should understand that *how* he answers may be different than what you request. Ask for that new car you've been craving and see if he delivers it to your doorstep. He might! Or your old car may give up the ghost and now you need to buy a new one. Voila! Prayer answered in a roundabout way. See how it works? (If you don't, that's fine. I don't see how prayer works all the time either.) So, ask for the help you need as a parent to raise your child and see how it develops. You could ask for patience, insight, wisdom, empathy, or understanding. Did I mention patience? Next, ask for your teen's sake—what does he or she need? Any of those same traits? Others? Like focus, thankfulness, sincerity, attitude adjustment, or hope? How about taking responsibility or showing respect? Ask away.

5. *Write them down and check them off.* Once you get the hang of it, don't be afraid of writing your prayers down. Not so God remembers them, but so that you do. When he answers—and remember, he may get creative in how he answers—you can check them off your list. Over time you will see how a kind and benevolent God takes care of you and fulfills your requests.

6. *Be daring.* Ask others to pray for you. Oh, boy, that's a big step, huh? You have to admit that you pray, that you believe in prayer, and that you need more help. Three biggies to confess. But if God hears the same prayer from many people—and be specific for what you need your friends to pray—think of the impression it will make on him. This is the concept behind a "prayer chain".

7. *Pray in front of your teen.* Don't worry, I'm sure they won't think you're crazy. Well, pretty sure. Just keep the prayers simple and short. Get in, get out. Don't belabor the point. And be sure to follow up with your teen when one is answered.

8. *Ask your teen to pray, too.* They may not carry the prayer

baton at first. But once they learn the power of prayer and see the results, they may jump on board. It may not happen overnight, but these things take time. Have patience. You've prayed for that one, haven't you?

If you pray, here are a few things that will happen:

- You will develop faith.
- You will begin to understand God and his ways.
- You will eventually want to serve other people. It will start with your teen, the one you already serve in so many ways as parents. But it will expand to your spouse, others in your families, and then to friends, your community—good, I think you get the picture.

Praying is not some hairy-fairy happening or hocus-pocus trick. It's a connection to the universe. Nobody knows the full power of prayer. We tap into a small portion. We hit a small vein of prayer gold. But look out! Once God gets behind you, nothing can stand in your way. Nothing can defeat you. Nobody can take away your power.

Parenting Tip

I have a notebook I started December 23, 2001. In it, I wrote down prayer requests I received either from my friends or relatives. They kept similar requests from me. I listed the day I began praying and the date I believed the prayer was answered. Now, in some cases, the answered prayer was not exactly what was prayed for. It was simply my interpretation of an answer.

As I look back on that list now—and I added to it through 2012—about 80 percent of the prayers have been answered.

Some, like a cure for AIDS in Africa, were pretty bold. Maybe God is still working on those.

My point is: God answers prayers. First you have to pray. Then you have to listen. And if you keep track, you might just be amazed at all the prayers he answers.

Amen!

If you feel you've been praying a very long time and God hasn't answered your prayers, I'd like to recommend additional reading. Laurie Polich Short wrote a wonderful book called *Finding Faith in the Dark* about her struggle to understand how God is present even when it doesn't seem like he's hearing your prayers. It gave me a whole new perspective on how to listen, see, and interpret how God works. Maybe it'll help you, too.

Parents Prayer

I know that I can talk to you about anything, Lord. I believe that your grace is way bigger than any guilt I may have. Open up my heart that I may lay all of my troubles and worries at your throne. Open up my ears that I may hear your voice— every day, all day. Guide me on the path that you have chosen; light the way for me—to you and for your glory. Thank you, sweet Jesus. Amen.

Stretch the Strategy

1.   Develop the skill to define your prayers in detail. (Read the best prayer books I know—anything by Stormie Omartian.)
2.   How would you describe your prayer life? How long and how often each day do you pray? How does that compare to others you know? If you don't know, ask them.

#4
Help Your Teens to Know and Use Their Strengths

"For I know the plans I have for you," declares the Lord, *"plans to prosper you and not to harm you, plans to give you hope and a future."*

—Jeremiah 29:11

God has a plan for your child. Your son or daughter wasn't born into this world simply to exist, like a cosmic placeholder until the exact right person comes along to achieve part of God's plan. Specially built and handcrafted by the master of the universe, your child will be used by God to the best of their ability for his purpose. It's part of *your* purpose as a parent to help them figure out what that is.

Sometimes I look back at my high school yearbook, usually when a reunion is in sight. I'll glance at the small summaries in the back of the book for the graduating seniors. Each summary lists activities the senior participated in during their time in school. My list includes writer, leader, sports enthusiast, achiever, and student. I like to think I'm still on course for those trajectories in life. So, the teen years are a great indication of developing strengths, gifts, and talents, and also a great opportunity to explore new hobbies and interests as an introduction to life. (We'll talk more in Chapters #23 and #24 about encouraging your teen to explore and develop interests.)

Life in its early stage—especially as children transition into teens—provides a great time for exploration. Many kids eagerly try new experiences, and as a parent, you can help them explore. As they grow older, they will recognize—with your help—what they like and don't like. That may lead to a discovery of their strengths, those attributes in which they readily and, in some cases, easily excel. Some will be brilliant in math, others not so much. Athletes, whether baseball players or dancers, can discover their talents and skills at an early age. An affinity for the English language, putting watercolors to paper, or building soapbox derby cars can illuminate a child's talents.

Some kids excel at many activities. Eventually, as the teen matures, parents can help them narrow down possibilities for the future—to use those strengths to pursue education, passions, and careers. This is a very important role that a parent, and often a teacher, play—a guide on the side.

My daughter loved to dance at a young age and trained with a local dance studio. Not only did she enjoy the camaraderie of friends, she also liked to perform. We talked a lot about how the practice of performing in front of a live audience would help her later in life. Although she no longer performs, she's had a successful career in public relations where her performance skills and a comfort level being in front of crowds serve her well.

Happy, successful people find ways to use their passions and their strengths in life. If you aren't using your strengths, you can languish and become discouraged. Many fine books exist to help discover your passions in life. (I used Nancy Anderson's *Work with Passion* and, when I was younger, Richard

Nelson Bolles' *What Color is Your Parachute?*) Most work well with young adults, and they can be tremendous resources for parents to help direct teens in their life's journey. If you need more insight, find and read these types of books and apply the strategies with your child. Each possesses tremendous insight and many practical exercises to help define an individual's passions and strengths.

Parents, if you're reading this and realize that you're not utilizing your talents and passions in life, it's never too late. Children will often mimic their parents and if you display unhappiness in the way your life turned out, why not use this time to join your child in this process? I dramatically changed career paths more than once after the age of 40. You can, too. Please jump in—the water may be a little chilly, but it's invigorating. (Nancy Anderson has written a book especially for you; it's called *Work with Passion in Midlife and Beyond.*)

Of course, not everyone can identify his or her strengths, especially at a young age. As a parent, it's your privilege to help your teen explore lots of different activities and interests, to expand the possibilities of what the teen may experience so they begin to notice what they're good at and what they enjoy. That's a good first step to defining strengths and talents. Naturally, we should help our kids work on their weaknesses, improve their shortcomings, and encourage the experimental or impossible, too. It's okay as a teen to experiment. I "experimented" with music as a youngster; it was helpful to learn that I had absolutely no talent or affinity for playing an instrument. Even when a child tries to accomplish what may seem impossible—and they fall short—they learn valuable lessons about perseverance and achievement. I certainly, at least, learned to appreciate others with musical talent.

Help teens learn to capitalize on their strengths. Teach them how a strength in one area of life could be used as they grow into adults. How a strong suit in math can lead to success in business. How an artistic flair can be used for a career in graphic design, product design, marketing, or as an artist. How a love of computers opens doors in the technology world. How a mechanical skill or a love of working with your hands can lead to well-paying, satisfying lives—and much needed jobs—in the crafts and trades.

One friend of mine told me a story as we discussed this chapter. He said that when his son was a teen, he was totally immersed in video games. At first my friend was wary of what, in his opinion, was turning toward obsession. Many parents have similar fears, I'm sure. My friend wanted to strongly discourage his son from this hobby—until he discovered the benefits. His son's affinity and talent for video games enabled him to reach out to other teens with similar interests. It allowed him to expand his social skills, inviting kids into his home to play—and talk and bond. I'm not saying we shouldn't be wary of the addiction to video games, but that we should not immediately jump to conclusions about interests and talents just because our initial reaction is negative.

Teach your children to see things as they are, not as they wish them to be, as it relates to their abilities. Your child may want to play professional basketball, be a movie star, or make it as a world-famous musician. Yes, they may be able to achieve any one of those dreams with hard work and training. Good for them—they should go for it. But if their strengths lie elsewhere, helping identify those talents will lead to less drama-filled lives and unfulfilled dreams. Don't deliver that small dose of reality as a dream killer but rather as a simple but important fact of life. Only a tiny fraction of one percent of people achieves greatness in those glitzy, glamorous professions. As a parent you can point, guide, and direct kids who haven't developed a maturity level needed to make long-lasting decisions. Of course, helping to develop a back-up plan with your child in case dreams dissolve is a great idea, too.

Encourage your child to be an explorer in life. To ask questions, investigate careers, to explore new hobbies, ideas, and…everything. Keep in mind, the skills teens develop during their formative years may indicate where their life will go and where impact and purpose will blossom. Artists. Engineers. Dancers. Writers. Plumbers. Painters. Carpenters. Anything you want to be. It's all available for exploration as a teenager.

To use your strengths—your God-given gifts and talents—is one of the central and most meaningful themes of this book. You'll see this thread in various chapters, including:

- #10 Encourage Teens to Have a Job Early in Life
- #17 Equip Your Teens to Take Constructive Feedback
- #18 Teach Teens to Recognize and Be Willing to Improve Their Shortcomings
- #23 Help Your Teens Explore and Discover Their Passions in Life
- #32 Show Your Teens the Benefits of a Lifetime of Learning
- #33 Help Your Teens Develop a Vision for Their Successful Future

I believe that God creates each one of us individually for a special purpose. No two of us are exactly alike—there has never been another you and there never will be. Unique and one-of-a-kind. He built us from scratch so we can fulfill that purpose in our lives, and we just need to find out what it is. Make it a journey, an exploration, a quest for buried treasure. Never settle for less than what you feel you were built for. Never.

As George Barna says in his book, *Revolution*, "Our relationship with God helps us comprehend the purpose of our life and defines the direction to pursue that will please Him and thus provide us with the greatest fulfillment."[1]

God sees us as perfect—that's the way he built each of us. We can become broken in this life, but we were not constructed that way. If we find the purpose for which God designed us, we will revert back as much as possible to that perfect being. Now that is a goal worth pursuing.

Parents have the opportunity and privilege to help prepare their teen to live a life using their gifts and talents. That produces happiness, fulfillment, honor, satisfaction, and purpose. If your child could experience a life like that, would you say you did a good job, parents? Who wouldn't want that for their children? Start now in the teen years to explore those possibilities.

Be sure to keep this theme handy in your parental toolbox. You'll use it often.

Parenting Tip

Go online and find a self-assessment test. Something your teen (and you, for that matter) can easily complete, without cost if possible. These evaluate personality traits, future job possibilities, emotional assessments, and the like. Start by googling "free personality test". (Parents, if you have these assessments about yourself, be sure to share them with your child—they'll love to know more about you.) Several that you might find useful are the DISC personality test, Jung's Personality Test (Myers/Briggs), Color Code, and the Murphy-

---

[1] George Barna, *Revolution*, (Tyndale House Publisher, Inc., 2005), 87.

Meisgeier Type Indicator for Children. Most of these are not free but the more well-established firms can help guide you through the process. Like most things online, do your research before you shell out money. You can always talk your child's teachers—they will offer great insight about your child's personality. "Learning style" assessments help identify the way a student learns most efficiently. Identifying this can give a teen power over his/her learning and exploration of topics. A school guidance counselor might be able to recommend other assessment tools as well.

Don't make a big deal out of what the assessment might reveal. Don't let the test pigeonhole your teen. Say something like, "It's only one assessment." Let the teen know they'll probably take more as they grow up. Use the test as a snapshot in time to help your teen understand themselves better.

Then discuss what the test reveals. Is it accurate? What's missing? Do you and the child agree with the findings? Be aware that you'll need to help your teen assess themselves throughout these discovery years. And remember to encourage them—to point out where they can use the strengths indicated in the test, both in their life today and in future careers.

Parents Prayer

Lord, teach me how to explore with my teen. Help me to put away my fear of change or new things. Show me ways to encourage and assist my child as he or she looks for new paths, new directions, and new possibilities. Guide me in exploring and identifying gifts and talents in my children and help make the process fun and exciting. Thank you, sweet Jesus. Amen.

Stretch the Strategy

1. How well can you identify your strengths and areas for improvement?

2. How well are you using your strengths in life? Are there changes you could make to better utilize your skills?

3. Discuss with your spouse each other's skills. Be kind. Don't spend time discussing "areas to improve."

#5

Teach Your Teenagers to Apologize

Make this your common practice: Confess your sins to each other and pray for each other so that you can live together whole and healed. The prayer of a person living right with God is something powerful to be reckoned with.

—James 5:16, *The Message*

When discussing this chapter with a friend of mine, she revealed a startling situation about her youth.

She said, "My parents told me never to apologize. That it was a sign of weakness."

I wondered how many hurts in her family went unacknowledged. Stuffed down deep inside, festering, maybe bubbling up later as anger...or shame...or worse.

I believe the exact opposite. I believe you show *strength* when you apologize.

Apologizing is not easy. If we apologize, we have to admit we are wrong about something. That's the hard part. Most of us don't like to admit we made a mistake or did something wrong. For some of us, it's almost impossible to make that admission; for others, it's a sign of weakness.

But apologies solve so many problems.

An apology mends small rifts. It can repair larger tensions. An apology can help recover relationships thought to be irresolvable. If coupled with a sincere "I love you," an apology can be the first step to solve almost every relationship breakdown. Jesus never demands that you have to be perfect, just that you come to him and ask forgiveness when you screw up. And he's always accepting of apologies, never disgruntled that it took too long to arrive or wasn't delivered with eloquence. Just that you said it.

When teaching kids the art of apologizing, as parents we should first model the behavior. (Just FYI, parents, that's another recurring theme throughout this book: parents modeling the best behavior. Just so you know.) You can apologize to your teen when you make a mistake, do something stupid or wrong, or simply mess up. You do not have to be perfect as a parent. In fact, when we make mistakes, we illustrate that we are human, and we give encouragement to our children that they do not have to be perfect either. That's a huge gift to kids, especially today. Many teens now get trapped in this pursuit of perfection. Perfect grades, perfect looks, perfect life, posted perfectly on social media.

For example, parents in some households apply much pressure on kids to get perfect grades—and even higher than perfect, above a 4.0 (yes, that's possible!) Many kids are held to such high standards that they feel they simply cannot make mistakes. That can lead to unbearable stress. They'll be enough stress for these kids when they reach adulthood; we don't need to bombard them with more at such a young age.

Listen, we *all* make mistakes. Newsflash: *nobody* is perfect. Please let that sink in a little bit. Take a deep breath and repeat it.

We all make mistakes, and nobody is perfect.

Whew…what a relief, huh?

Now, back to apologies. First, find small mistakes you make as parents and learn to apologize to your children for them.

- Maybe you forgot something they told you
- Maybe you spoke harshly to them for no apparent reason
- Maybe you had a bad day and took it out on them
- Maybe your punishment was ill-advised or a little over the top

Whatever the reason, find it and apologize for it.

Then ask your child if they forgive you. They will, don't worry. Then forget about it and don't bring it up again. If your child mentions it, tell them that they forgave you so it's a done deal. A dead issue. No takebacks, no reviews (unless something was unsaid or miscommunicated.) We want to teach children that once an apology is given and accepted, life moves forward, that we don't have to keep rehashing old mistakes and we shouldn't be forced to feel bad about those mistakes or continually apologize for them.

Of course, children may not forgive some mistakes we make as parents. We'll talk more about forgiveness in the next chapter. And you may need to give the child a little time to accept the apology. Even small missteps by parents can be hard for some children to forgive. Just keep apologizing with sincerity and asking for forgiveness. If your family is struggling with issues that cannot be resolved through heartfelt conversation, sincere regret, and humble apology, you may need to seek out a counselor to help you. Please don't let these struggles fester and go unresolved.

Here's a personal example when I had to apologize to one of my children. When my son was a teen, he had a hard time channeling his emotions on athletic fields. He was hyper-competitive and if things didn't turn out his way, he lost his temper and had outbursts of anger. After one high school basketball game that his team lost at the buzzer when the opponent my son was guarding scored the winning basket, I met him outside the locker room after the game. He was almost in tears and trapped in anger and guilt. I came down way too hard on him to control his emotions. (In my lame defense, it had been something we were working on.)

He tossed an f-bomb my way and shoved past me, walking away. No others heard what he said, but I was mad. I didn't like being treated that way and I didn't like how he spoke to me. So, I thought he should be reprimanded. The next day, I talked with his coach about possible penalties.

But it was the wrong time, the wrong place, and the wrong criticism from me.

After I realized he'd been caught up in the moment and was sorry for his actions, I knew he didn't deserve any further punishment. Then I apologized. *I was wrong, bud, I screwed up. I should have given you time to cool off. Will you accept my apology?* He did.

It was not one of my shining moments as a dad, but luckily, I'd learned the particular technique of asking for forgiveness in my marriage. Many, many times. Okay, that's another story. (Repeat after me: *We all make mistakes, and nobody is perfect.*)

As a side note: my son learned to channel that emotion

into energy and competitiveness and earned a scholarship to play Division 1 college football. Mostly his nature and a bit of our nurture.

Next, find a small something that you think your child could apologize for. If your teen hasn't been taught the art of apology, don't begin with a whopper of a mistake. Don't make the first apology something monumental. They can practice this skill and build up to that. Make sure it's a very recent incident.

- Maybe they forgot to clean their room like they promised.
- Maybe they spoke harshly to you, just because.
- Maybe they had a bad day and made you pay for it.
- Maybe they treated their younger sibling badly.

Don't go back in time for more than 48 hours. Don't dig up the past looking for something. Teach them to say the words, "I apologize, I'm sorry." Make sure there is sincerity in their voice, because at first, there may not be. You learn this sincerity skill; it doesn't necessarily come naturally. Modeling this skill with sincere language can be a powerful tool for parents.

Then, accept the apology and tell them you love them, and they are forgiven. End of story. Let's move on. And do not, I repeat, do not bring up that particular incident again. Let it go. We should *not* be teaching our kids that they need to continually apologize for something that has been forgiven. That will only teach them *not* to apologize—for anything. Now, if they keep making the same mistake and keep apologizing for it, you may have a behavior problem. A key part of accepting an apology is making sure the child corrects the behavior.

A word of caution: some kids will devise clever schemes to

use an apology to cover up bad behavior. They think that if they apologize—and some do this with dramatic sincerity—Mom and Dad will be blind to the offending behavior. Don't fall for this one, parents. If you see your child offering up unsolicited or frequent apologies, it may be a warning sign that you need to dig a little deeper.

Keep setting the example by apologizing to your kids. And enforce the benefits of having them apologize to you. Please remember, you don't have to use the word 'confession'. That sounds criminal, like confessing to a crime. Apologize is the right word—it's softer, gentler.

Once children and teens learn to apologize, it's not such a big hurdle to jump over. Once everyone learns to forgive, life moves on without all the baggage of hurt feelings, tarnished relationships, and lingering resentment. When teens learn to apologize, humility becomes a part of their personality—and being humble will serve them well throughout their lifetime.

In today's world, humility as a personality trait takes a backseat to more powerful, forceful characteristics like strength, endurance, and persistence. But the benefits of humility are coming more and more to light. Recent psychology studies have found that forgiving, humble people have:

- Lower blood pressure
- Lower bad cholesterol and resting heart rates
- Improved sleep and immune systems
- Less depression, anxiety, and anger
- Enhanced relationships
- More optimism
- A greater sense of overall well-being

One study even showed that after forgiving another person, you can actually jump a little higher. Maybe it's because you're carrying a little less weight.

We'll continue this discussion in the next strategy, accepting apologies and forgiveness.

Parenting Tip

Kids enjoy seeing how their parents solve marital problems. So, parents, find a time in your relationship that you apologized to one another. Share the actual event that needed the apology, the response of the spouse that received it, and the feelings of the one delivering it. If there was reluctance to apologize, be sure to tell your kids that, too. It's important to let them know that apologies are not always easy, but if they can see the end benefit—and the techniques used to confess—they can visualize the lifetime advantage of this important strategy.

For single parents, use this idea with a relative, a close friend or a business associate. Preferably somebody your child knows. (This is the modeling I was referencing above.)

Parents Prayer

Lord, humble me to confess and apologize. Let me be the example of a forgiving and forgiven person. Take away my pride of being right or righteous. Tender my heart to forgive others without retribution or regret. Thank you, sweet Jesus. Amen.

Stretch the Strategy

1. How did your family handle apologies when you were growing up? How has that shaped the way you view this strategy?

2. Is there someone in your life that you need to apologize to? What's prevented you from apologizing?

3. If someone has passed away that needed to hear an apology from you, please apologize. In prayer, out loud, in your heart, to Jesus—find a way. Assume they'll hear it, someway, somehow. Confide in your spouse how you apologized. Heal the hurt by apologizing.

#6

Teach Your Teens to Accept Apologies and to Forgive

Bear with each other and forgive one another if any of you has a grievance against someone. Forgive as the Lord forgave you.

—Colossians 3:13

Once you have taught kids to apologize, teach them to accept others' apologies and to forgive. There may not be a more precious practice between two individuals than the act of forgiveness. Again, it may not be easy at first. Sometimes we want to hold onto our grudges because, *"Well, they were wrong and I was right and they should feel bad about it—at least for a while."*

If you have practiced forgiveness in your household since your kids were little, you've got a good foundation to build upon. If you taught siblings to share toys, clothes, or food, you probably had an instance where you had to teach one of them to forgive the other for stealing something from their brother or sister.

Practice this with your spouse in front of your teenagers, too. Find actions you can apologize for and accept forgiveness between the two of you. This sets a great example for your children and teaches them the power of forgiveness.

Parents, here's a short list of times in your marriage when an apology might have been delivered and accepted. You can probably add more. (If you can't think of more, check with your spouse!)

- I forgot to include you in a decision
- I didn't help out around the house like I promised
- I was late for dinner and didn't call
- I left the kitchen (or the bedroom or the den) a mess when I left the room
- I forgot to record your favorite TV show
- I erased your favorite TV show
- I spoke harshly to you
- I didn't tell the truth
- I thought you could read my mind
- I didn't take your feelings into account
- I should have known better
- I'm an inconsiderate dolt at times
- I got way too emotional

Next, find something your teen needs to apologize for. We talked about this in the previous chapter, but it's worth repeating. Here's the key: don't go looking for mistakes. Just be aware of them in case they happen. Of course, you've probably laid the groundwork so that your child knows what's expected, so these hiccups will not come as a surprise to you.

In raising a child, one main responsibility of parents is to teach right from wrong. But kids often lose sight of these boundaries. Especially in today's American culture where they are influenced in so many different ways. Kids don't call it relativism—this blurring of the lines between right and wrong.

They say things like: "What's right for you may not be right for me."

That is almost verbatim a comment my son made to me when he was a teen. An eye-opener, for sure. It opened up a continuous conversation between the two of us about how he was coming to a conclusion about what was right and wrong. He never said this, but I suspect his friends influenced many of his opinions, especially at an early age. It is a common occurrence for teens to be more influenced by their peer group's opinions and less by their parents' beliefs, however it doesn't make it any less frustrating for parents.

No, sorry, that's not how it works. Not on the basics, like telling the truth, being kind to others, and being fair and just. It might work in politics or business where gray areas emerge, but right and wrong at home, for the basics, is black and white. As parents, you establish these boundaries. You don't have to be a harsh and relentless enforcer, but the more you apply the rules of right and wrong with your teens, the better prepared they will be to deal with the nuances and gray areas they'll encounter as they grow older. Build the foundation when they're young.

The Bible contains many great examples of right and wrong, especially as it pertains to teens.

- Loving your neighbor vs. shaming, ridiculing, or laughing at them
- Helping others vs. only looking out for yourself
- Trusting God vs. trusting yourself, your friends, or other influencers
- Practicing humility vs. exhibiting selfishness or righteousness

The Bible provides a great resource for instruction. Lessons learned by Biblical characters can illustrate what went wrong, how God intervened, and how course corrections in life turned out (good and bad—either one teaches a lesson.) But if you only use the Bible to teach right and wrong, your kids may think you're some kind of religious zealot. Be sure to also incorporate present-day situations that reinforce your points. It's a great mix of instruction, and your children learn to deal with everyday issues with practical examples.

Maybe your teen made a mistake in one of these common occurrences below, where they have been taught right from wrong, but stumbled.

- I forgot to clean my room, or the bathroom, or (fill in the blank)
- I didn't do my chores
- I spoke harshly to you
- I spoke harshly to my brother or sister
- I lied
- I bent the truth
- I lied by omission, not telling you something I should have
- I didn't tell the whole truth
- I didn't keep my word or my promise
- I disrespected you
- I disrespected my brother or sister

When they apologize for the misstep, forgive them with a generous heart, not holding their mistakes against them. Shower them with big hugs, big kisses. Tell your teen that you love them no matter what. Nothing they could do is unforgivable. Nothing. Nada. Zilch. End of story.

Let me reiterate a point I made earlier. Don't go looking for mistakes or keep lists of potential mistakes. Your child—and your teen—will supply you with enough room to work. There will be no shortage of them. And don't point out every single mistake your child makes. Nobody likes to be hammered with continual criticism. In fact, make sure you point out as many, or more, *good things* your child does, too.

It's a delicate balance, but it's teaching right from wrong. *This is right, congrats, good job. That is wrong, I think you should apologize or accept another's apology.*

Once they apologize, accept it and tell them they are forgiven. When you apologize and ask for *their* forgiveness, make sure they have granted it. A shoulder shrug, a sullen nod, or an exasperated eye roll could mean they'll hold onto that grudge a bit longer. Maybe a smile and a sincere "I forgive you" won't happen right away, but it's a target to shoot for.

Again, let me emphasize, I'm talking about issues that most of us face regularly in families. If there are bigger problems in your family—those that cannot simply be apologized for and forgiven—then you might need to seek professional help. Remember, if a child keeps seeking forgiveness for mistakes made repeatedly, that's the red flag to dig deeper into why the behavior has not been corrected.

The traits of apologizing when you need to and offering forgiveness at every opportunity will help instill in a child an open, caring heart, willing and able to accept, embrace, and love others without hindrance or hang-up.

Parenting Tip

This may be a good time to open up a discussion with your teen about "right and wrong." It's going to be a strategic conversation you engage in with them. The more you express your standards of right and wrong, the more it's synched with their thinking. For instance, some families think that underage drinking is always wrong. Other families let teens share a small glass of wine occasionally at dinner, like many families do in Europe. If wine is not taboo, their thinking goes, maybe the teen will not be so lured by it.

We will explore this theme of right and wrong often in the book. So, it's a good time to talk with your spouse to begin compiling a list of what you, as parents, think about right and wrong. If you are a single parent, confide in friends with teens and compare notes.

Here are several topics to get the ball rolling—to first discuss as parents—and then with your child:

1. Is cheating on an exam acceptable? Under what circumstance?
2. Is lying okay? How about a little white lie? How about lying to your parents? To teachers? On your income taxes? (Oh, the places we can go with this conversation, huh?)
3. If something is illegal, like underage drinking, is it always *wrong*? Why or why not?
4. Now list a few right/wrong issues important in your family...

Parents Prayer

Dear Lord, make me a forgiving person. Give me a spirit of grace. Fill me with your spirit daily and hourly so I see my spouse and my children through your eyes. Allow me to love them with a warm and tender heart. Thank you, sweet Jesus. Amen.

Stretch the Strategy

1. How easily do you forgive? Share and discuss with your spouse.
2. Is there someone in your life that you need to forgive? What's preventing you from doing that? Can you forgive them? If so, how?

#7

Build a Non-Critical Spirit into Your Teens

How can you say to your brother, 'Brother, let me take the speck out of your eye,' when you yourself fail to see the plank in your own eye? You hypocrite, first take the plank out of your eye, and then you will see clearly to remove the speck from your brother's eye.

—Luke 6:42

Most of us have an inner voice that speaks to us. Sometimes it's classified as your "nature" or simply just "how you are." It influences you, for instance, in how you react to circumstances (*this is scary* or *this isn't so scary*), how to view the world (*out to do me harm* or *full of opportunities*), and how to speak about other people (*negatively* or *positively.*) Of course, happy mediums exist in any of those situations.

But being critical of others is not necessarily natural. I believe it's a learned behavior. And it's most certainly utilized in America these days to its most ugly extreme. Because of its prevalence in culture and media, your teens may think this is acceptable behavior.

Maybe *your* parents were overly critical—always with an

opinion, a crack about somebody or something, or a dig, jab, or put-down. Perhaps you socialize with friends who always want their voice heard and, more times than not, a critical streak emerges.

Maybe you believe that God is critical, too. That the Bible is simply a book of rules and if you don't follow them, God's wrath comes hot and heavy. But God is not a joy stealer; he's a joy giver. As Joyce Meyer says, "Watch out for the joy-stealers: gossip, criticism, complaining, faultfinding, and a negative, judgmental attitude." The God I read about in the New Testament, embodied by Jesus, is none of those.

Criticism exists as a double-edged sword—it can be positive or negative. I'm talking about the bad aspects of criticism here. Of course, teens need to learn to express their opinions. They need to voice their side of an argument. They can disagree. It's good for them to develop a back-and-forth dialogue with others. I'm concerned here with teens being mean and judgmental, cruel or uncaring, nasty or callous. That kind of criticism reeks of the unhealthy and misguided.

Have you noticed that some people like to criticize? It's almost a game with them. "People watching" quickly turns into a game of shame. *Let's point out everything we don't like about that person—shoes, hairstyle, face—even though we don't know them.* With today's social media, it's easy to hide behind a wall of secrecy or a fake identity—and it's common practice to voice criticism without consequence.

Other people have learned to praise instead of criticize. Or, at the very least, to hold their tongue and not say (or post) anything at all.

When my son played youth baseball, I became friends with the father of a boy one year older than my boy. I knew the person currently coaching this man's son would coach my son the following year. I asked my new friend how he liked the coach. He looked at me, opened his mouth, closed it, contemplated some more, and eventually never said a word. Not. One. Word. His silence conveyed volumes about his feelings, but he never said a bad word about that coach. That was over twenty years ago, and I still remember it as a great example.

Some teenagers like to tease, to make fun of others, and to point out what's not cool. When they get in groups, they can single out others and pummel criticisms in the form of "put-downs"—a barb, a dig, a slight, a sneer, a snub. These comments tend to shame or belittle the recipient and leave them hurt, deflated, and maybe depressed. This is one form of bullying—being a bully with words. This behavior often indicates the bully's own insecurity. They feel the need to belittle others. Something about being in groups of teens escalates this behavior.

Of course, adults fall into this trap, too. So, the first order of business in this regard is to watch *how you speak about others*, parents.

For instance:

- Do you criticize your spouse?
- Do you belittle those you work with?
- Do you gossip about your friends or acquaintances?
- Do you criticize your pastor or his sermon or the worship music in church?
- Do you criticize yourself?
- Are your comments really criticisms disguised as "opinions"?

Maybe you don't realize you're doing this. It's easy to get caught in this trap. It's actually quite fashionable in some circles—like cable TV news programs. But you can always shift your perspective and find something good to say. Maybe now is a good time to start and be a good example for your kids to follow.

When you hear your children criticizing—that mean, judgmental slant—stop them, too. Point it out and let them know how it might make the other person feel. If they criticize you—and they probably will at some point—let your kids know how it makes *you* feel. (We'll talk about expressing feelings in a later chapter, so stay tuned.)

The digital world, especially the world of social media, does nothing to curtail criticism. It actually makes it easier because you can't see the impact of the pain of the poke. You won't notice the hurt in the eye or the slump of the shoulders.

The same rule applies for digital dialogue as for actual dialogue: if you can't say anything nice, don't say anything at all. (There have been so many times recently when I've wanted to post a snarky remark on Facebook and had to stop myself. Not always, but mostly.) If your children are not used to this practice, it might be a hard transition for them, so you'll need to be consistent—and persistent—with feedback. (Even *facts* today are debated, so this argumentative, critical culture we're living in will definitely make this discussion challenging for parents. Just what you need, right? Another challenge.)

As Dr. Wayne Dyer writes in his landmark book, *What Do You Really Want for Your Children*: "When you see children beginning to form opinions about everyone and everything without the benefit of any knowledge or study, encourage them to become more open and inquisitive. Remember that to simply have an opinion about a profound subject such as poverty, hunger, nuclear war, prostitution, religious wars, or anything else, is really quite trivial. But, to have a commitment to ending these problems is a profound statement about yourself. Teach children to make commitments rather than to simply have opinions. And also, teach them the shallowness of having opinions based on prejudices and a non-inquiring mind."[2]

When your children learn to tone down this critical attitude, relationships will shift around them. They may develop more friends because they'll become friendlier. In order to have friends, you must learn how to be a friend. Parents model this behavior by how they develop and act towards their friends. Kids may also have a better relationship with their teachers because they'll treat others better and teachers notice things like that. They may develop a sense of fitting into this world because they'll learn to see the world as friendlier instead of meaner and darker. And there may be less tension and drama around home because everyone will be a little less snarky. Oh, thank heaven!

The teen years can be hard, overwhelming at times. Stressful. I get it. Sometimes when you're close to the boiling point, you just want to yell…something, anything! Take a deep breath; try not to cry out with a criticism. The hardest part of all of this may be for you, as parents, to have a little time to think about what you want to say because it just wants to come out and often, it's critical. I know it was for me. If you ask my adult children, they'd probably say I was too critical when they were growing up. I'd like to think I'm learning to be less so. Of course, I don't spend much time on Facebook or Twitter anymore, and that helps.

I confessed in my book *Lumberjack Jesus* how I used to be super critical when driving my car. I thought it was a safe place to voice criticism because only my family could hear me. When

---

[2] Dr. Wayne W. Dyer, *What Do You Really Want for Your Children*, (William Morrow and Co., New York, 1985), 64.

I realized I did as many stupid and reckless things driving my car as others did, I toned it down. I'm doing my best to see other drivers who may be older, lost, confused, or who just prefer to drive differently than I do. I probably need to apologize to my kids for all the years before that epiphany. Sorry. And I still slip up. Sorry again.

It seems like in today's world, everyone's a critic. Everyone has an opinion—and more times than not, it has a streak of nasty included. Stop, already. Give it a rest. Tone it down, filter it out. Be cool, don't be cruel.

Eventually, your kids will thank you for it.

Parenting Tip

Confession time again, parents. I would like you to confess a time in your child's life when you were too critical of them. It's a form of an apology. It doesn't have to be a huge criticism; it can be minor. I don't want you to give up all your power in the teen/parent relationship, but I do want you to critique yourself. (Don't confuse "criticism" with discipline. Kids need discipline.)

You can also reverse this. You can point out a time in your child's life when they were too critical of you. It works both ways, doesn't it? Teens can be very critical of their parents— even to the dramatic conclusion that, "I don't love you anymore!" Sometimes they simply convey that criticism with a dramatic eye roll or head shake. Even the tone of their voice (like the fashionable retort, *"whatever"*) can convey nastiness, can't it?

Try your best to work it out. Discuss those moments and how you could have handled the situation, the criticism, differently. Your child may or may not be able to tell how they would *prefer* to receive such feedback—that takes a maturity level they may not have reached yet. But as a parent, you will begin to understand how each of your children is unique in this regard and how they handle feedback differently.

Parents Prayer

Sweet Lord, help me to hold my tongue and to have a less critical spirit to my fellow man. Guide my language and thoughts, especially around my spouse and kids. Let me see the good in people, anticipate the best, and expect goodness in others. Thank you, sweet Jesus. Amen.

Stretch the Strategy

1. How often do you express opinions without sufficient facts to back them up?
2. Can you hold your tongue during times of heated discussion? Can you walk away? Do you see those as signs of weakness or strength?
3. In what areas of life do you need to speak less and dig deeper to discover the truth?

#8
Teach Your Teens to Contribute to Others

Not all of us can do great things. But we can do small things with great love.

—Mother Teresa

We make it all about us. We put ourselves in the center of the story. We evaluate life from the vantage point of a scary and tragic 'me-ism.' We pull the border of our concern into the narrow confines of what we want, what we feel, what we dream, and what we think we need. A good day is a day that is pleasurable or easy for me. A good circumstance is one in which I get my way.[3]

—Paul David Tripp

T he 1980s in America epitomized the "Me Generation." Remember the movie *Wall Street* with Michael Douglas and Charlie Sheen? It illustrated the concept of making

---

[3] Paul David Tripp, New Morning Mercies, (Crossway, Wheaton, IL), 2014, p. 8/3.

as much money as you can for yourself—no matter the cost to others. I'm not sure much has changed.

Have our attitudes about money changed? Attitudes about what constitutes success? About giving or contributing to others? Do you see much difference in the greed and self-preservation in the Me Generation and how life is lived today? Looking out for #1—that quality of putting me first—hasn't dimmed all that much lately, has it?

Sometimes things just stay the same.

Take teenagers for instance. They probably aren't much different today than in the past. An aura of self-centeredness seems to seep into the teenage years, at least to some degree. These young adults want to establish their identity, their own path, their future, their skills—and that focus can be all consuming.

It's not necessarily misplaced. We *want* our children to do all those things.

It can just be a little much at times, right? It's fine to look out for yourself. But it's noble to care for others.

Sometimes teens think about their friends and relatives, but often, they think about themselves first. Please don't get me wrong. There are some wonderful teenagers out there in the world doing great things for other people. I suspect they had terrific parental influence.

Many teens learn to contribute to others from their parents. People they see in the news may influence them, but if they don't see their parents contributing to others, they may not pick up the habit.

Oh, my goodness—it still comes back to being the example, doesn't it, parents? Ask these questions of yourself to see how you compare as givers, as contributors.

- Do you give of your time and talent without expecting anything in return?
- Do you volunteer locally for a charity or non-profit organization?
- Do you serve somebody, like an elderly neighbor or a single parent, just from the goodness of your heart?
- If you attend church, do you tithe? How much—ten percent or more?
- Do you support a child overseas in a poverty-stricken country on a monthly basis?
- Do you believe that all you have has been given to you and that you will leave this life as you entered—with nothing?
- Do you have a heart for the hurting?
- Do the sufferings of the world that break God's heart, break yours?

So how might we teach our kids to have a heart for those less fortunate? Besides being the example and sharing with your children how you contribute, how can you soften the hearts of the young, so they see more than their individual wants and needs? A few suggestions:

- Spend a Saturday every month, or every quarter, in service to other human beings—anywhere.
- Find a neighbor that needs help. Maybe an elderly friend needs a lawn mowed, leaves raked, or snow shoveled. Have your kids do it for free, no charge, out of the goodness of their hearts.
- Seek out those less fortunate than your family and show your kids how differently they live from the way your

family lives. Is it a homeless shelter? A recovery house? A drug halfway house? "The other side of the tracks"?

- Find a family project for contribution. Collecting food for a local food bank is a great idea. Involve your friends and neighbors. Set a huge goal: Five hundred items of food, maybe more. Deliver the goods to the pantry and ask to stay and help them distribute to less fortunate families.

- Adopt a family at Thanksgiving or Christmas. Maybe your church could help plan this through an agency in your town that helps underserved families. At Thanksgiving, it could include supplying the dinner with all the trimmings. At Christmas, you may be able to help with gifts, school supplies, clothes, meals, or gift cards. Do your research, fulfill the need, and make a difference.

- Buy fast food gift certificates in five-dollar increments. Let your kids give them to disadvantaged people, like the homeless, they see on the streets. (Of course, you want to do this safely, and parents should always accompany the kids.) You don't have to make your kids buy the certificates with their own money. The impact comes from simply seeing, and contributing, to those less fortunate.

- Take a supervised "mission" trip with your family. This can be coordinated by a church or simply through a travel agency that specializes in visits to remote places. Visit Mexico, Haiti, or other parts of the world that might be classified as "underdeveloped." Spend a few days or a week, eat the food provided and experience the poverty that exists. It will open your eyes—and your children's—to the privilege and responsibility we have as humans to care for the entire world, not just our households or neighborhoods.

- Let your teen come up with an idea for a project in contribution. It will look great on their list of high school achievements and their college applications. It will also teach organization, recruitment (they'll need help), and management, and instill a huge sense of "making a difference." We all want to make an impact, and it's never too early to start. (In fact, in some school districts there is a requirement for graduation that the student participate in some form of service-learning project and report about it as part of a senior project presentation.)

Talk and reflect about these ideas with your teens. Start with questions: inquire about how they feel about those less fortunate than themselves, what they saw, why they think the condition exists. Point out when you see inequities in the world. Try to stay away from blaming somebody for the problem; that can get you lost in the blame game. Just point out how fortunate you and your family are compared with others who didn't get the breaks you did. Even if you consider your family unfortunate, there will be examples of families in other countries who are way less fortunate than you.

When I was a young father with teens in the house, I worked hard at my job and was committed to the future of my family. But I didn't involve my kids much in contributing to others. I missed this opportunity. I suspect your kids are already WAY too busy with life—soccer practice, homework, dance lessons, math tutoring, learning to play the saxophone—and you don't need ONE MORE THING to add to the family agenda. But I could have done a better job working less and teaching more about making a difference in the lives of others.

Learn from me on this one—voice of experience talking here.

I'm not saying, parents, that you both have to quit your jobs and move the entire family to Haiti to serve in a remote village. (There *are* families that do that, though. Just imagine!) Maybe carve out an hour a month to give back. Just shifting the focus off us for a tiny bit of time can make a huge difference—in our lives and the lives of others.

Renee and Craig Janofski's story illuminates one family's dedication to others. After making several trips to Haiti as short-term missionaries to an orphanage on the Haitian island of La Gonave, in 2013 the husband-and-wife couple quit their jobs in the United States and moved to Haiti. For the first two years, the family, including their two pre-teen kids, managed an orphanage of a hundred children and trained the staff. Craig's expertise is systems, management, and technology; Renee excels at fundraising, social media, and teaching. After completing that project, they moved on to Extollo International, a nonprofit dedicated to helping Haitians rebuild their country by training in construction skills, among others.

Living in Haiti can be brutal. The poorest country in the Western Hemisphere, the left half of the island of Hispaniola was devastated by multiple hurricanes in the 2000s and an epic earthquake that killed an estimated 250,000 people in 2010. The process of rebuilding the island, which has little infrastructure and minimal building standards, can be frustrating. Yet the Janofskis fight on. After six years, they left Haiti recently for a year sabbatical. They vow to return to continue the progress. Their constant flow of stories of Haitian lives changed bless their family and many others beyond what most of us could comprehend. To help change an entire country keeps them engaged, committed, and blessed. Their kids now exhibit this sense of contribution.

If you can find ways to instill a sense of blessing on your

teens—and if they live in the U.S.A., they are way more blessed than most—they may see how awesome it is to bless others. There is no better way to live a life that matters. If you can instill this early in the lives of your children, imagine the impact they will have throughout their lifetimes.

Parenting Tip

Devise ways to open your children's eyes to what is happening in the world. This is especially crucial for those kids who grew up privileged or "spoiled." In California where I live, teens often talk about growing up "in the bubble." It's a comfort zone around them where they don't see much outside that zone. Take kids outside their comfort zone. For example, have them visit soup kitchens in the inner city (or better yet, have them serve in those kitchens). Have them serve the homeless during Thanksgiving. Accompany them as you hand out healthy snacks or toiletry items to the homeless. Help them develop a servant's heart to those less fortunate. This will take much planning and teaching. There are nonprofit organizations that have systems and services in place in which you and your child can participate. You don't have to do this all on your own.

If you live in the inner city and your kids see this every day, you might have to work a little harder. You may need to find places that are worse than yours. I've been to Haiti, where most people live on less than $2 a day, so examples exist out there, believe me. Find ways—maybe online is your best bet—to show your kids that no matter how tough their life is, somebody has it tougher.

Bonus Tip: Okay, this one is a little out there. On a Saturday, give your teenager $2 and tell them they have to live on that for the day. You won't be supplying meals; they can't raid the frig or mooch off their friends. (This may take a little coordination with other parents, I know.) It will be fascinating to see how they sustain themselves for three meals. You can have a sumptuous dinner planned for later that evening but don't tell them.

The point: they will not be able to buy much of anything with that $2. They'll be hungry. Maybe frustrated, even mad. But they might begin to understand the principle.

Take it a step further: tell them they also have to find water for the day; they can't use any source in the house. (Many kids in underdeveloped countries spend eight hours daily just trekking water.) Have a little fun with this experiment; it's just one way to get the lesson across. I'm not advocating we starve or dehydrate our kids—just presenting a teachable moment.

Parents Prayer

Dear Lord, soften my heart for others that are hurting. Show me what breaks your heart that it may break mine. Make me the kind of parent that sees the needs in the world outside of my family. Help me to engage my family in contributions to others and help me build that spirit into my children. Thank you, sweet Jesus. Amen.

Stretch the Strategy

1. Discuss with your spouse how well you contribute to others as a family. Do you have resources to expand your contributions?
2. If you don't have many resources, how could you develop a plan to contribute to others that doesn't cost much money?
3. What spiritual practices soften your heart for others?

#9

Encourage Your Teenagers

A 'please remember' is always better than a 'don't forget.'

—Joy Crough, Preferred Performance

New experiences fill the teenage years—and at times they can come fast and furious. Dating, learning to drive, school demands, jobs, college prep, and extracurricular pressures can be overwhelming for some kids. Even if your teens don't seem to get stressed by it all—and some hide that stress pretty well—they'll need lots of encouragement. Not misplaced or constant praise when it's unwarranted, just plain and simple encouragement.

You remember the teen years, right? You panic when you can't find a date to the prom, stress out for the big biology test, feel devastated when you experience a broken heart—and pimples! I broke out in a sweat just writing and remembering all that.

Here are some other words for encouragement that may help you get the picture:

- Help
- Reassurance

- Inspiration
- Cheer
- Praise
- Reinforcement
- Support
- Backup
- Boost

You can always offer a safe harbor of support to your teenager. There shouldn't be any subject that you can't talk about. Sometimes just listening is all the encouragement they need. As teens try to find their way in the world—and you know it can be a scary world today—they need parents who are simply "there" for them. All the time, every time. To listen, to understand, to empathize, and to nod that you "get it".

One way to offer encouragement is to focus on effort and perseverance rather than simply results. We want our teens to know that giving their "best effort" means something to us as parents. We're proud when our teens do their very best, almost regardless of the outcome. Learning to work hard toward a goal is valuable, even if you fall a bit short.

"Perspiration can outwork talent" is a good life lesson.

In other words, encouragement phrases like "run the race" and "don't quit" and "stay the course" and "give it your best shot"—even though they're all clichés—can push a teen beyond what they might expect of themselves.

When men and women of the Bible became overwhelmed with the tasks laid out before them—often at God's direction—he always encouraged them. Abraham, Jonah, Moses, David, Ruth, Mary—it's a long and indiscriminate list. Overwhelm can affect even the most determined and focused. When God gave his people tasks that they judged as impossible—leading an entire nation from bondage, building an ark to house all the animals of the world, rising up alive from the dead—he was there to support and encourage.

Here's a much less awe-inspiring example from my family. My daughter started first grade before she was six years old, so she was usually the youngest in her class. For several years, she always felt behind the rest of her classmates in schoolwork (and she *was* sometimes)—and that often overwhelmed her.

Everyone else understands this and I don't! It seems easy for everybody else but not to me!

Until she developed the maturity to stick with a school project even when she was frustrated, she needed lots of encouragement.

She needed:

- *Yes, you can do this.*
- *I know it's hard, but you can figure this out.*
- *You'll be fine; just keep working.*
- *We're here to help you.*

My son needed fewer pats on the back. He had a slightly stronger ability for self-encouragement. Sure, he needed praise, and my wife and I did our best to deliver just enough. I hope we didn't under encourage him. But as his accomplishments grew, especially on the athletic field, we wanted to be sure he didn't get too full of himself. We managed to keep that balance—most of the time. I think. It's always a balancing act.

Now let's spend a little time on overdoing it in the praise department. We all know parents whose children can do no wrong, but did you ever meet a perfect child? Children who are always told they are perfect never learn to see the faults in themselves, only others. When parents build a child's self-esteem up to the point the child actually perceives that they can do no wrong, then we are surrounded by kids who don't understand constructive feedback. When another person points out a child's misstep, like a teacher or a coach, then the child becomes flummoxed. *But I can do no wrong, isn't that what my parents say?*

It *is* a balancing act, isn't it? How do you encourage without spoiling? How do you accomplish encouragement without overdoing it? Or, maybe just as harmful, underdoing it? A child that gets little or no encouragement may see most everything as daunting and overwhelming. These rules to remember ring true:

- *When the teen is downcast, sprinkle encouragement. When the teen is full of pride, temper encouragement.*

- *When the teen is unsure, encourage without restraint. When the teen is too sure, rein in encouragement.*

- *When the teen is faced with a big challenge, build them up. When they have no challenge, offer up a few.*

- *When the teen needs a boost of encouragement, give a cheer. When the teen needs a dose of reality, deliver the reality news.*

- *When the teen weakens from doubt, offer support and reinforcements. When they stand too tall from their own pride, point out the other side of life.*

It's up to you, as parents, to determine the need and deliver the dose. And it's okay to deliver that dose. A dose of reality, of humility, does wonders for the younger child and miracles for the teen. Remember, good medicine rarely harms the patient, even if it tastes a little awful going down.

(Are you hearing Julie Andrews right now singing "just a spoonful of sugar helps the medicine go down"? Maybe it's just me.)

What if we only encourage? Is that so bad you ask? I say again, everything in moderation. Do all sports participants really need a trophy? If everyone gets a trophy every time, no matter how well or poorly they participated, how will they ever learn to be champions? If champions play for trophies—that's another pitfall, isn't it?—and at the end of the contest, everyone gets a trophy, what do champions have to play for?

Teach your teen to accept encouragement and to know when it's true and heartfelt—and when it's hollow. They'll figure it out pretty quickly. My son always knew when an over-enthusiastic athletic coach was blowing too much smoke his way. Of course, he figured out that coaches can be over-dramatic and hypercritical, too. Just don't let *your* encouragement be hollow. Constant encouragement, when unwarranted or overused—just like criticism—can eventually land on deaf ears—an insincere message indeed.

Parenting Tip

Document your encouragement. Short, handwritten notes given to your child with an "attagirl" or an "attaboy" are treasures. Many kids keep these and refer to them at times when they need a boost. Suggest ways that they can store these treasures—a special box, a journal, or a drawer in their desk. Maybe a file folder they keep in a secret place. It's a "Feel Good" file—and it's always available when they need encouragement. I still have one that I started for myself thirty years ago. It's filled with not just words of encouragement from others, but "success" projects I completed at various times in my life that still make me smile today.

And words matter, too. The quote I opened the chapter

with (please remember is better than don't forget) epitomizes the need to put words in the positive, rather than the negative. Your brain works better with 'remember' and can short-circuit with 'don't forget.' So, remember that, got it?

Parents Prayer

Jesus, help me to distinguish when my children need encouragement rather than criticism. Guide me in the right words to say in every situation. Help me to rely on you when I don't know exactly the right path. I want to lean on you because I know you want the best for my family and me. Thank you, sweet Jesus. Amen.

Stretch the Strategy

1. Are you an encourager or a criticizer? Discuss with your spouse.
2. How did the way your parents raised you affect the way you use praise and encouragement?
3. Discuss with your spouse the phrases you typically use, both positive and negative, that may affect how you convey lessons to your kids.

#10
Encourage Teens to Have a Job Early in Life

The plans of the diligent lead to profit as surely as haste leads to poverty.

—Proverbs 21:5

When is the right time in life to look for your first job? Maybe the answer lies in the question "why work when you're young"? Let's jot down a few reasons why teenagers should jump into the job market:

- Jobs teach responsibility.
- They teach us to be on time.
- Jobs foster self-respect.
- A job well done elicits praise, a self-confidence boost.
- Jobs teach us that we continually need to learn new skills.
- When working, we know who the boss is—always a good lesson in life.
- Jobs teach us to take direction and correction.
- Jobs demand that the teen learns time management. Everything still needs to get done.
- Jobs build your history, your resume in life.

- Jobs teach the benefit of team building. Most everything in life happens on teams.
- Most jobs teach you to pay attention to detail. If you don't, you may not keep the job.
- Many jobs encourage ingenuity. Sometimes the boss isn't around and it's up to you to figure it out.
- Jobs allow the teenager a bit of financial independence and savings skills.
- And here's one you may not have thought of: that first job is a great time to instill the trilogy of having money! One, save some; two, enjoy yourself with some; three, give some away to another more needy. That's a great lesson to teach.

Are there any downsides to teenage jobs? Sure...

- Jobs can take time and energy away from studies and schoolwork.
- Bad jobs and bad bosses are plentiful in the world. We've all had one or the other, haven't we?
- Some jobs are just plain horrible—and you don't learn much of anything at all.
- Teens can be taken advantage of in bad jobs. (Be sure to check out the U.S. Labor Department's website, youthrules.gov, for rights of underage workers.)

Oh, I know what you're thinking. Teens are way too busy to work; their plates are too full. Or they have too many pressures, what with schoolwork, heaps of homework, extracurricular activities. How in the world could we add joining the workforce onto the pile? Isn't that just too much to handle?

We had the same concerns in our family. My daughter got

her first job at sixteen and always had a job, even during the school year. She thrived. My son played three sports in high school and earned a college scholarship to play football, so he never had a traditional job until after college. But sports taught him all the great lessons that having a job does. And his "job" was earning that scholarship. (No, I'm *not* saying that girls should work and boys should play sports, so don't even go there. My daughter played all the sports and then became a wonderful dancer.) We saw both sides of the argument.

Jobs teach life. Teens need to learn about life as much as they need to learn about succeeding in school. (Go back and read that last sentence again.) Sure, being in a good school teaches many of the same lessons as jobs—responsibility, respect, new skills, team building—but can you rely on today's schools to deliver all that? Some do, some don't.

If you decide that a job is right for your teen, they'll probably need help landing their first one. Parents can offer suggestions for types of jobs, how to apply, how to interview (if there is one), how to be enthusiastic, and how to land and succeed at the job.

It's more difficult now for teens to find jobs than in the past. According to the research nonprofit organization, Child Trends, the number of high school students who work has dropped from a peak of 35 percent in the 1990s to 18 percent in 2015. They attribute the decline to automation, international competition, and teens increased focus on academics. Unemployed adults have also slipped into those traditional teenage jobs. Coupled with the "Apply Online" instruction for many openings, it's hard for teens to land a job even in retail stores or fast-food restaurants.

Parents will need to help teens stand out in that marketplace. Here are a few tips that will come in handy.

1. **Develop their communication skills:** When a job opening only offers an online application—as more and more do these days—help your teen develop a phone conversation to use to encourage a prospective employer to interview them in person. You might try role-playing the interview. Cue to teenage eye roll. I know, it's awkward and embarrassing, but it works.

2. **Help the teen make a list of references** to use in the interview or application process.

3. **Inquire with your connections**—friends, relatives, and work associates—to see what jobs are available for your kids. (It's still *who* you know.)

4. **Help your teen practice an introduction** of themselves when they first meet a prospective employer. (Thirty seconds, including their interests, skills, and assets.) Remember, you never get a second chance to make a first impression.

5. **Teach your teen to follow up** any opportunity with a physical, not a digital, thank-you note. (So, they'll need to get all the right information…correct name spelling, address, etc.)

Then, when your teen lands the job and it progresses, you'll need to get daily updates by asking lots of open-ended questions. Dear Parent, don't settle for the answer "fine" when asking your teen how the day at work went. A one-word answer is no answer at all. Mostly, "fine" and "okay" are conversation stoppers. *Don't ask anything more.* Kids have the knowledge to make accurate details of distinction all the way from "exquisite" to "excruciating" so don't accept something aimed at the mediocre middle so you'll just quite asking. Consider it a teaching moment to allow your teen to communicate. If the job is bad, find that out and find out why. If there is trouble on the job, help to distinguish where it's coming from and who's responsible for cleaning it up.

I'm not a big fan of having jobs in your own home. Emptying the dishwasher, mowing the lawn, cleaning their room, setting the table, and all the chores around the house that make up daily living are *not* jobs. They're contributions to the family, and all kids should have some responsibilities in that regard. An allowance? Great idea. An allowance with strings attached (like completing their chores)? Another good idea. Extra jobs that need doing that you can financially compensate your child for: okay, find them. Washing the car provides a great opportunity. But don't let them get away with a poor job. Any job worth doing is worth doing well—that's a great lesson to learn.

And remember, it's hard to be a boss and a mom or dad at the same time. If you're paying your child for work around the house, set the expectation and requirements and don't let them slack from those. But be a nice mom or dad, too. No bullhorns or bullwhips to shape your child into a slave laborer, please.

Not all jobs are great and not all bosses are good. Your teen may need help making good job choices. That's an important part of life. Quitting a bad job can lead to finding a good one. So, help your teenager decipher the good ones from the bad.

And finally, help them understand what they're learning on the job. Not the little details of stocking shelves, mowing grass, or changing dirty diapers, but the core learning of responsibility, respect, and others from the list that started the chapter. That's a job well done for you, parents.

Parenting Tip

Be sure to talk to your teens about jobs that you had as kids. First of all, your children will love to hear about your teenage years. Include not only jobs you hated, but also ones you liked. If you can remember, mention how much you made per hour. As I recall, my first job, washing cars on my dad's used car lot, paid me $1.25/hour. And since he was my father, I'm sure that was above the going rate. Maybe some of you had paper routes where you had to get up before dawn, no matter what the weather. Be quick to point out the lessons you learned because most jobs at that age are menial, and it can be hard to see the lesson amid the mundane. Make this a fun stroll down memory lane; don't fill it with cruel, hard life lessons learned. Not like this: "I had to walk a mile to my job, through six feet of snow, uphill each way."

Bonus Tip: Technology can be confusing for adults who grew up watching black and white TV or using rotary dial phones and manual typewriters. But to many teens, technology is fun and exciting. Perhaps your teen is a tech whiz. I imagine people would pay handsomely to have their phones fixed (or explained!), their computers running smoothly, or their software programs deciphered. I think that's a job opportunity worth exploring for your teens.

Parents Prayer

Lord, my life can be filled with to-do lists and anxieties. Help me to relax and depend on you. Guide me as I teach my children the benefits of work and how to prioritize a great work/life balance. Open my eyes to see what work my kids can do and how they can enhance their education through a job. Thank you, sweet Jesus. Amen.

Stretch the Strategy

1. Did you work as a youngster? Can you see the benefits or working when young that you didn't see at the time?

2. Discuss with your spouse, friends, church groups, and others your views of working during the teen years.

3. When viewing your own children, do you see working as a teen as burdensome or beneficial? Why? Articulate your reasons with your spouse.

#11

Show Your Teens What a Good, Strong Work Ethic Looks Like

Passion Secret #3: Powerful people know that getting there is all the fun.

—Nancy Anderson, author of *Work with Passion*

Let's not leave work and jobs quite yet. There's a little more to say. Remember, I'm not writing about finding a career, pursuing your life's passion, or fulfilling your dreams. It's just a job, at least for now in the teen years.

When teens get their first job or two, the learning curve ramps up. Now dad and mom can help explain what's expected and what any employer prefers. Of course, expectations should come from the workplace, but we all know they often don't. "Be on time and do a good job" is not a detailed expectation. It's a start, but it's too basic. Help your teen figure out those unexplained expectations. Let's begin with these:

- Be on time, maybe even early.
- Do a good job. (Sorry, I couldn't resist.)
- Show up every day. Don't make excuses not to go to

work.

- Don't call in sick unless you're really, really sick. Or contagious.
- If you don't understand the job, ask for an explanation of the task.
- There's not much you can't be asked to do at the job—within reason—if you start at the bottom.
- Be courteous, especially to customers.
- The customer is always right.
- The boss is always right.
- Enjoy your work. If it's not enjoyable work, at least look like you enjoy it.
- Ask to do more than what's expected of you.
- Never talk bad about the boss behind the boss's back.
- Never talk poorly about the job. Especially to other employees, customers, or the boss.
- Never lie to the boss.
- If you are expected to look nice, smell nice and be nice, do those.
- Never get high or intoxicated before or during the workday. (I'm sorry I had to say that.)
- Develop a good attitude. You are probably going to work for 40 years or so; and hopefully you find work that fills you with joy with passion. But you may not right away so learn to enjoy what you're doing now.
- If you don't enjoy the work, see it as a learning experience.
- Learn to understand the importance of perseverance—sometimes you just have to work harder (and smarter.) But sometimes, it's just working harder.
- Add a few more of your own.

Parents, teens often have first jobs that are not challenging, pay poorly, and that can be downright bleak. Remember back to your first few jobs. Great lessons can be taught during these times.

The first one is obvious:

Get a good education so you don't have to do this kind of job for the rest of your life.

The second one is less so:

Learn as much as you can at any job, so that you can move up the ladder to the next job.

The third, even less so:

Every job needs done, so you might as well do it well and have a good attitude about it. (That's a nice life lesson, too, isn't it? Don't complain—get on with life.)

Sometimes American teens have trouble transitioning between being with friends and being at work. Think about it; as adults we rarely have to do such a bipolar transition. Maybe we jump between job and family, but we have responsibilities in both arenas. When teens are with friends it's all fun, it's all the here-and-now, it's sassy, and sacrilegious. Then they have to show up for the job—and it's none of that. If they act the way they do with their friends, they probably aren't doing the job. They'll be reprimanded or scolded or chewed out or fired—all of which can hurt and be unexpected. Here's where you come in parents. Teach them how to do the job!

Parenting Tip

I worked another job as a teen on the "detail rack" in my dad's auto dealership or as we called it, the "garage." This was much worse than washing cars. It entailed taking used cars and detailing them so they looked as good as possible before they went to the used car lot. Nasty work in the summertime in Pennsylvania in the back of the garage that was not, I repeat, was not air conditioned. Here was my day. Somebody, usually my older brother, picked me up at our house at seven forty-five a.m., Monday through Friday. I punched a time clock, and my day began at eight a.m. I would wash the car, dye the floor mats their original color. Sometimes wax the car or buff out scratches with the auto buffer. Or paint the wheel wells and reattach the hubcaps. (I know, I'm dating myself, but you can teach your kids what cars were like in the old days with this example.) Often, I would degrease the engine with a nasty smelling product and then paint the engine. The list of what a used car needed became endless. And did I mention that in the humid summers of Pennsylvania that the garage was not air-conditioned? Punch out at five p.m., and I'd try and find a little energy to have fun with my friends in the evening.

Now it's your turn parents. Describe a job that required a work ethic above and beyond. Long hours, little pay, backbreaking work. Don't be afraid to lay it on thick. And don't just concentrate on menial jobs. Many vocations that require a college education can be downright draconian. But it's good that they know. It'll teach them what it takes to succeed, that everyone has to start somewhere, and it'll emphasize the importance of finding a lasting career that they'll love.

Parents Prayer

Heavenly Father, help me to trust in you, to trust that you want the best for my family and me. Teach me to live each day for you—to live knowing that you are in charge. Change my attitude from one of dread to one of delight. Help me to see each day as a gift and help me to teach this to my children. Thank you, sweet Jesus. Amen.

Stretch the Strategy

1. Do you love your work, your career? How much?
2. Are you following your passions in life? If not, what's next?
3. What would you as an adult be willing to sacrifice (time, money, salary) to pursue a new career, a new passion?

#12
Teach Your Teens to Thank Others

The more you're thankful for, the more you realize how much you have to be thankful for.

—Bruce Kirkpatrick (and probably many other people)

This may not come as a surprise to you, but teenagers can be a little self-centered. No great revelation there, right? Duh. We've discussed that it's a time for identity building and discovery, so a little bit of selfishness should not be a big cause for worry or concern. But we want to raise kids to have caring hearts and respect for others. What's one way—maybe the best way—to balance those dichotomies? Teach them to thank others (and to *Give Others Credit*; I cover that in #13 next.)

Remember the text from 1 Thessalonians 5: 16-18,

Rejoice always, pray continually, give thanks in all circumstances; for this is God's will for you in Christ Jesus.

What does thanking others teach?

- First and foremost, not to take credit for everything yourself
- To be humble
- To think of others
- Basic manners
- Being polite
- To put a smile on somebody's face
- To make others feel good
- To do the right thing
- That others contribute to you
- We are all in this together

Here are a few examples of things that teenagers can thank others for:

- Presents
- Advice
- Money
- Homework help
- Straight talk, honest talk
- Constructive criticism, like a teaching moment (That's a tough one, huh?)
- Driving teens places
- Preparing meals for teens
- Cleaning the house or doing the laundry or folding the laundry
- Teaching teens to be happy
- Respecting their opinions (You do, don't you?)

- Having their back, backing them up
- Not being too hard on them, especially when they deserve it
- Being hard on them, especially when they deserve it (Another tough one.)

Parents, you thank your teens when they contribute around the house, don't you? You thank your spouse when they deserve an attaboy or attagirl, right? You set the example for your teen in this arena, am I correct?

If you respect everything that people do for you around the home, then giving thanks is a natural follow up. If your teens regularly thank you as parents—for big contributions and smaller ones alike—then you're well on your way to raising responsible adults. If you notice your child has to be coaxed, prodded, or threatened to thank others, you have work to do. Find ways to instill this small, but vital, trait into your child.

A few ideas:

- Compile a list for what requires a written thank you and when a verbal or digital thank you is enough.
- Supply them with thank you notes and stamps.
- Give them a reasonable time frame to complete a thank you.
- Suggest ways to verbalize their thank you.
- Provide ideas for written notes.
- If an email or text message is appropriate—for closer family members and pre-approved by the recipient— make sure your kids know the protocol. Emails and texts are not always suitable.
- Follow up with your teens in a fun, lighthearted way to make sure the thank you was delivered. No guilt trips,

unless absolutely necessary.

- Set the right example.

I know I'm a little old-fashioned about written thank-you notes. In this age of text messages and email, a digital thank you can be perfect. It's easy and quick. Just be sure the expectation is met. If somebody expects a written thank you, remember, they will never go out of style. And your child will stand out from the crowd who only send digital thank you messages if they send a written note.

I see one troubling trend beginning to develop in America. Do you know those little goody bags some younger children receive at birthday parties? The ones filled with small gifts that children receive as a thank you for coming to the party. Often included is a preprinted thank you note that the child can return to the host. All they need to do is sign it.

What a great idea! On the surface, at least.

But children miss the lesson of giving thanks if all the work is done for them. *Here, sign this, and I'll send it back,* says the parent. What has the child learned? Not much—the thought of the thank you is forgotten almost instantly. It's much better, parents, to give them a blank note—and offer help or suggestions of what to say—so they can write their own thank you. Can you see that this is a good habit to teach?

I thought so. Good job. Now expect nothing less from your teenager.

Honest confession: We have two kids. One regularly sends hand-written thank you notes to express gratitude. The other one, not so much. We can only do our best, right?

Okay, let's talk about the corollary to thanking people in the next strategy, which is giving credit to other people.

Parenting Tip

Thank your spouse out loud in front of your kids for something they do for you. Make this practice a habit. You could even make a list and write it down. Maybe you come up with ten things your spouse does for you in which you are thankful. A *Top Ten List of Thanks*. Then hand it over in front of the kids and review it with everyone. I don't have to give examples here, do I? Type it up and make a big deal out of it. Tack it up on the frig. Review it every so often, for instance, twice a week. After a month or two, devise a new list. Now you'll have to dig a bit to find thankfulness. Perfect, that's the point of the exercise.

The more you're thankful, the more you realize how much you have to be thankful for.

And that's the lesson we want to teach here.

For single parents, this list may be what your *kids* do for you for which you're thankful.

Parents Prayer

Teach me, sweet Lord, to have a thankful heart. Help me to show gratitude first to you for all you have given me, for all you provide, and for all you *will* provide. Instill in me an attitude of gratitude, showing my children the power of thankfulness. Help me to find unique ways to express my thanks and make me the kind of person who readily reverts to thanking others before patting myself on the back. Thank you, sweet Jesus. Amen.

Stretch the Strategy

1.   Do a little research in your Bible on the topic of gratitude. What did you find?

2.   Do you regularly thank Jesus for all that he's done, all that he's doing, and all that he will do in your life?

3.   Are there people in your life, like coaches, mentors, bosses, family members, that have contributed to your life that you haven't thanked—or want to thank again? Devise a plan to do that.

#13

Teach Your Teens to Give Credit to Others for Their Successes

For by the grace given me I say to every one of you: Do not think of yourself more highly than you ought, but rather think of yourself with sober judgment, in accordance with the faith God has distributed to each of you.

—Romans 12:3

Nobody makes it on their own in this world. It's impossible. Forget the old notion—there are no self-made men or women. There never were. Make sure your kids understand this because it seems like many American teens believe they are somehow isolated from receiving help to figure out their future. Sure, some people are more independent or self-sufficient or they prefer to work alone. But no man—or woman—is an island. All right, enough with the clichés. (But they work, don't they?)

When many children enter the teenage years, they cross a threshold. Many crave at least some separation from their parents. It's a natural thing. Eventually, most will want to disconnect and move into their own life. They want independence; and when you think about it, they deserve independence. Good, that's the way it's supposed to happen. If they can gain some independence from Mom and Dad and still stay tethered to God, all the better. They take on more responsibility. They assume more control. They adapt to the transition.

But they should never lose sight of the contributions of others, starting with their parents. They may have to be taught this trait—giving credit to others—because as they begin to cross that threshold, they can get a little full of themselves, a little self-centered.

But why give others credit? How am I going to instill self-esteem in my child if they give others recognition? My first answer is: Don't overdo the self-esteem. Too many teens have too much self-importance and not enough humility. Help them find the balance between being confidant and being humble.

Here are a few reasons teenagers should learn to give others credit:

- They will need that ability later in life: on the job, in marriage, and with children of their own.
- Giving credit to others shows respect.
- Giving recognition boosts the other person.
- The teen will feel good, too.
- It's one clear trait of leaders who gather a loyal following.
- It's a unique and heart-warming trait, especially in young people.
- Giving others credit enables teens to stand out among the crowd—from other teens who don't.
- It shows that teens are not just thinking about themselves.

- It builds humility into their personality.
- It's *always* the right thing to do.

Now let's list a few examples of when and where this can work:

- When complimented on athletic ability, a teen can say: "My mom (or dad) is really athletic. I get a lot of my athleticism from them."
- When acknowledging academic achievement, a teen can say: "My folks (or teachers) taught me lots about studying. Plus, they're both really smart, too."
- When their good manners are noticed, a teen can say: "My grandparents (or parents) really emphasize manners. They taught me everything I know."
- When doing something nice for another and being noticed for it, a teen could say: "They've done a lot of nice things for me in the past. Just evening up the score."
- When complimented at work for a job well done, this might sound pleasant: "Thanks. I've learned a lot from many people around here to make my job easier."
- If a group project at school earns good accolades, a teen can give credit to the group: "It certainly wasn't just me. Everyone did a great job."

Do you understand how these remarks and reactions will make the parents of these teens feel? Grandparents, siblings, bosses, friends? And can you see that this type of teen would attract others to be around him or her?

Both of our kids participated in team sports. That's a great environment to build this character trait of giving others credit.

As parents, we always emphasized the contributions of others on the team to its success, especially if *our* kids had great games. Absolutely, give kudos to your kids—and make sure you spread the credit around.

Believe me, giving credit to others can be contagious. If parents practice it around the home, teens will pick up on the idea. Teens learn by observation and parents are directly in their observation sights. If you remind them why we give credit where credit is due—it's not humiliating, it's enlivening, it's invigorating. If they slip up or get jealous of the success of others, just correct with a soft heart, not a critical spirit.

Ask them how they feel when somebody gives them a compliment. Voice how you feel when they complement you. Show them with a smile or a chuckle or a "thanks, right back at you" reply. It's contagious! And it feels so good.

This is the fundamental human spirit—a way to bond with others, a method to boost not break down. Humility can open the door for empathy and compassion. When you see others through these eyes, it softens your heart. It can rid you of a callousness that is isolating. In this American era of mettlesome meanness and unbridled disrespect, this trait of giving others credit will set your teen on a course not many see and fewer will take. A course of reconciliation and unity. A path of resilience to the contempt of today and a blueprint for tomorrow's responsibility.

We'll need young adults with that personality in the future. We need them right now.

Parenting Tip

Talk to your children about somebody you admire. Maybe it's your parents or your grandparents. Tell stories about your childhood and how individuals contributed to you. Maybe you had a teacher who took a special interest in you and helped you develop above and beyond their job description. Give specific examples of what you learned.

I often told my kids about my maternal grandmother, my "Dan Dan." She had the most incredible ability to be happy. Nothing seemed to faze her or trouble her. She would walk down the streets of our hometown literally whistling a happy tune. Extremely embarrassing at times for me, but also it was a great example of injecting a positive attitude into any circumstance.

Your kids will not only love to hear more stories of when you were young, but they'll easily pick up on the impact of these people in your life. My kids did—to this day, they thank me for the contributions I still make in their lives.

This is a great time to sit and talk with your teen about this chapter. How does it make them feel? What are their ideas about giving others credit? How can this work for them? Do they see the benefit—or do they need more examples?

(Side benefit: if you haven't thanked these people who made such an impact on your life, now is the perfect time. It'll be another great example for your kids, too.)

Parents Prayer

Thank you, Lord, for everything you have given me. Thank you for the sacrifice of your son, the pain he suffered, and the death that he endured, so that I may have life. Help me to never forget all that you did for me. Humble me at your feet as I confess my lack of understanding and fulfillment. Make me the thankful and generous person you've envisioned. Thank you, sweet Jesus. Amen.

Stretch the Strategy

1. Do you agree with this strategy? To give others credit? How did your upbringing contribute to your view of this?

2. Do your regularly, parents, thank your parents or grandparents for their contributions to your life?

#14
Teach Teens to Smile and Laugh

Hearty laughter is a good way to jog internally without having to go outdoors.

—Norman Cousins

D o you know somebody who always smiles and laughs? Are they fun to be around? Is their smile and laughter contagious? Doesn't it make *you* a little happier just to be with them? Are you smiling just thinking about them right now?

You've probably heard some of the benefits of laughter, like:

- Releases endorphins, the body's natural painkillers
- Boosts the immune system
- Reduces stress
- Lowers blood pressure

And two you may not know about:

- Improves cardiac health (It's a workout for your heart!)
- Works your abs (Always a good thing, but who knew?)

Some people come upon a life of smiles and laughter quite naturally. It's innate; they're born that way. They received a major dose of happy when God assembled all the ingredients. Norman Cousins literally wrote the book about the healing power of laughter, *Anatomy of an Illness: As Perceived by the Patient.*

But some people and some teenagers struggle expressing joy. They don't smile much and laugh even less. It may be their nature, or it may have been their nurture. But they don't have to live that way forever. Nothing lasts forever; this too can pass.

My kids were lucky that they had a mother who almost always functioned in a good mood. My wife taught me much about expressing happiness. Her natural demeanor looked to the positive, in almost every situation. Thanks, hon.

What tactics will get teens to smile and laugh? Try these out for size:

- Smile and laugh yourself. Learn to laugh *at* yourself, too.
- Tell a joke. It doesn't have to be a good one. Bad ones count, too.
- Watch funny, stupid movies. Let the teen pick the movie. *Blazing Saddles* might be funny to you but not your teenager.
- Observe standup comics. Try to keep it clean; but a little potty humor may work, too. (I like Steve Harvey, Jim Gaffigan, and Ellen DeGeneres.)
- Tell funny stories of your youth.
- Find a funny book to share or read excerpts out loud. Dave Barry's *You Can Date When You're Forty* might be a

good place to start.

- Find a board game that your kids enjoy. Something quick that makes them laugh like Pictionary or Charades—or something more in their generation.
- Come up with a list of funny alternative names for farts, burps, and butts. Works every time, especially with boys. (See *Blazing Saddles* reference above.)
- Make up lyrics to your teen's favorite songs.
- Assign your teen to find "the funniest YouTube video of the week". Make it an assignment. Maybe a top five or ten every week. Share with the family.
- Find videos of animals doing funny things. View as a family. (The things we make our pets do, huh?)
- Share funny text messages you can find on the internet.
- Make a list of funny things boys do. And funny things girls do. Be kind!
- Come up with your own fun ideas.

One caution: don't find humor that laughs *at* somebody. People do funny—even stupid things—that can be humorous. But teens cans slip into "making fun" of people. If you find ways to laugh about yourself, and have the teen laugh about themselves, that's along the right track. Laughing at someone can quickly turn mean. Laughing *with* someone is much better. Know and use the distinction. Also, don't encourage examples of humor where someone is doing something where they get hurt. I'm thinking of some of the popular TV shows and movies trending now. You know the ones I mean.

Parenting Tip

Have a "worst joke of the week" contest. Find bad jokes every day and share them with the family, maybe at dinner time. Try to keep it clean, for the most part. Tell bad jokes every day, keep an informal list on a sheet of paper, then at the end of the week, vote which is "worst of the week." Remember, teen humor will be different than yours. You, as parents, may think that *all* their jokes are bad, and in turn, they may think *none* of yours are funny. But that's all part of the game. Good jokes are intended to make you laugh, and even bad jokes can make you groan.

If this runs its course—and it probably will—you can move onto other "best" categories.

- Best joke
- Best video
- Funniest video
- Funniest dog video
- Funniest cat video

The list is endless. Just be creative and let the belly laughs begin.

Bonus Tip: Teach your kids to smile at people. Just smile. There doesn't have to be a reason. If people smile back, great. If they don't, what have you lost? Make it a game: how many people can you get to smile back at you in a day? (You smiled when you read that, didn't you? And you felt better when you smiled, huh? Smile more.)

Parents Prayer

Lord, make me smile. Show me all the lovely nuances in life that delight you. Help me to turn away from darkness and turn toward light. Open my eyes to see all the good in you and in your people. Lighten my load so I may laugh at my mistakes and chuckle at all the things that I used to frown upon. Thank you, sweet Jesus. Amen.

Stretch the Strategy

1. Do you smile more often than you frown? Ask your spouse if you're not exactly sure.
2. What makes you smile? How can you incorporate more of what makes you smile into your life?
3. How can you remind yourself to smile more often? (Plug it into your calendar, use a sticky note.)

#15
Teach Teens to Find Humor and Fun in Life

The best way to cheer yourself up is to try to cheer somebody else up.

—Mark Twain

Some teenagers experience life with a sense of dread. They dread school. They dread the cruelty that friends heap on them. They worry about the future. They even fear many things that you, as parents, don't even know about. This is a time in their lives, as we've discussed earlier, when they can be independent, apart, even silent. Face it, you don't always know what's going on in their teenage brains. Dread is a terrible way to go through life.

For instance, teen suicide rates have been steadily climbing over the last decade. And in 2015, those rates hit a forty-year high for teen girls.

That's one reason these strategies about smiling and laughing contribute so much to the life of a teen. Piggybacking right along: finding humor and fun. We have choices how we live our lives. We can wallow in dark and dread, or we can seek the bright side. Help your teens choose the better way.

Be sure that teens learn to find the humor in their teenage years—to learn not to take life so seriously. Teens can face enormous pressure in the 21st century—pressure to be a success, to achieve the highest grades, to get into a good college, to find the perfect job, to date the perfect person, to be happy. Parents can contribute to that pressure. The rules of social media can force kids to only display a perfect life—and that in itself is pressure to always be, if not perfect, then almost so.

Teens need to learn to laugh at themselves. If they find humor in the ridiculous things they do and say—and believe me, there will be no scarcity of either—then they might not be so eager to poke fun at others. Or be so self-critical that they think about suicide. When they fall into the trap of criticizing or making fun of others, gently remind them of all the funny things they have done. Maybe keep a list someplace if that's not too over the top. I don't mean keeping score or making a long, detailed list of all the mistakes they've made. Just a short list of all the funny things they've done. These become the "family stories" that you can look back on after a few years and laugh. I'll let you be the judge of how to make this work. If your child is overly sensitive about this, back away a little. But realize that oversensitivity is simply thin skin. They'll need thicker skin in this game of life so that everything does not become so *dramatic*. OMG, the dramatics of American teen life!

Now a caution: don't raise teens that put themselves down. Sometimes it can be a fine line between laughing at yourself and being way too hard on yourself. Don't raise kids who think they're dummies. Raise kids who can laugh at their mistakes and not take themselves too seriously.

You can be the example here, parents. We discussed apologizing earlier. Now let's discuss laughing at yourself a little more around your children. Parents don't always have to be perfect, know everything, and be the upholder of rules and regulations in the family. Kids can learn from parents that the ability to laugh at yourself and find humor in missteps contributes to a life of joy.

Here are a few of my stories—times I did funny things that I can now laugh about. (Maybe not so funny at the time!) Admit it, you probably have similar ones. When I was young I:

- Mistook the slightly overweight neighbor as being pregnant.
- Mistook the female sibling of a good friend as her brother. (She *was* wearing a baseball hat and flannel shirt, after all!)
- When going to the front of the class to give my first presentation in a college music class, I ran directly into the piano. (Ouch on so many different levels.)
- Fell asleep in church and started to snore.
- Fell asleep at a concert! (Judy Collins—so serene. Beer might have been involved.)
- Couldn't remember the password to my phone. The one I input twenty times a day.
- Stumble with today's technology: programming the TV, operating the computer or the phone, wondering how to post to Pinterest, wondering what happened to MySpace.

Okay, now that I've got you started, make a list of your own. Get your kids laughing at your missteps and laugh right along with them. Make it a game. Just remember to emphasize that you're laughing with your kids, not at them. And they're laughing with you, not at you.

Laughing with somebody is fun. Laughing at somebody is just plain cruel.

Here's a fun idea. Create a "give somebody a break today" game in your family. Members of the family who make mistakes, especially goofy ones, get a "pass." *Okay, we'll let them off the hook for that one. Big eye roll, big smile.* If it's somebody in your immediate family, they have to laugh—or at least smile—along with everyone else. If it's somebody outside the family, assume they're laughing at themselves and just "give them a break today."

Don't make such a big deal out of goof-ups, blunders, "duh" moments, oopsies, bloopers, and slip-ups.

Can you see the fun in this? Life doesn't have to be taken so seriously, does it?

Parenting Tip

Did you see my blunders in the text above? Yes, I mistook a female as a male. (Haven't we all?) I ran into that piano—the embarrassment was much greater than the pain. I fell asleep listening to Judy Collins live in concert. So now it's your turn, parents. Reveal the unsightly. Quit hiding your goofs. Confess your imperfections. Your teen will find these examples hysterical. Believe me, any chance they get to laugh at Mom and Dad doing something stupid or dumb or goofy will have them rolling in the aisles. Don't be afraid of confession—it'll be fun for you, too. And you will show that we are all human and make mistakes. Hey, there's that theme again.

We all make mistakes, and nobody is perfect.

Parents Prayer

Lord, help me to be more cheerful, anticipating all the good things you have in store for me. Help me to cast my eyes on you when my attitude may shift to worry, dread, or despair. Show me you love in very tangible ways. Talk to me and make me listen to your voice. Show me to path to happiness. Thank you, sweet Jesus. Amen.

Stretch the Strategy

1. Are you too hard on yourself? If so, why? If not, how did you learn this?
2. Is it easy to laugh at yourself? What's one thing that you do that you could learn to laugh about?

#16
Help Your Teens Keep Their Promises

If you keep your word, no matter what, it teaches you perseverance, determination, and respect for others.

—Me, again

I didn't designate one of the numbers on this list of 33 strategies about telling the truth. Something like: "Always tell the truth. Never lie." That's just a little too obvious and elementary. Of course, you're going to teach that. As parents, we encourage our kids to be truthful. We teach them to never lie (or cheat or steal.) Fine, keep that up. Always emphasize the importance of honesty.

Keeping promises adds a few nuances to that foundation. One, it teaches teenagers to think *before* they make a commitment. If they practice keeping all their commitments—and they get burned every once in a while, because they make too many—then they learn to not overcommit in life. It's fine being busy; in fact, keeping teens busy just may keep them out of trouble. But teens also need downtime, and over-commitment robs from that.

What down time allows:

- Time to rest
- Time to reflect
- Time to wonder
- Time to plan
- Time to dream

I like this rule:

It's better to under-commit than to overcommit and not keep your promises.

Right or wrong, some people judge you on your word. If you can't keep your word—your promise—you are deemed unreliable. That's just the way the world works. We all know individuals who promise many things and rarely keep those promises. We tend to depend upon them less and less. Giving lots of promises—even with good intentions—without keeping them reveals a form of insincerity, a phoniness.

From Joshua 23:14: *Now I am about to go the way of all the earth. You know with all your heart and soul that not one of the good promises the Lord your God gave you has failed. Every promise has been fulfilled; not one has failed.*

God keeps his promises to us, even when we don't initially understand how he's done it.

Here's another truth that keeping promises teaches:

If you keep your word, no matter what, it teaches you perseverance, determination, and respect for others.

If keeping your word entails strife and hardship on your part—and you keep it anyway—that's something to build on.

You did it! Even though it was painful for you, you put the other person first, keeping your promise to them. Congratulations!

Now what happens if you give your word and then you realize you cannot keep the promise? Time to renegotiate. For example, if a teen promises that they'll mow the yard on Saturday but finds out later that they have a homework assignment due the following Monday and they need to research on Saturday. I'd rather see the teenager come back to the parent early on, as soon as they understand the over-commitment, and ask for an extension. *The assignment is due Monday; could I mow the yard after school that day?*

Of course, renegotiation has its limits. Not everything can be renegotiated, and if that tactic is used too often, it becomes just another excuse for not keeping your promises. But it can be used effectively, and if the parents judge the negotiation legitimate, letting the teen re-commit can be a strategy that exudes both kindness and mettle. Give the teen a break, and let them keep their promise, just at a later date. A win-win.

Here is a little pet peeve of mine. People who are always late. Just bugs me. I suppose there are times when it's warranted. I understand. But c'mon: be on time for goodness' sake. Is being late anything more than not keeping your promise? I know, I know, some people are always late. *It's just my nature,* they say. No, I say, if you're always late that shows little regard for my time or me—it's disrespectful. Obviously, I still need to work on my patience—we all have things we work on, right? Just in case you thought I was perfect. I can hear my wife laughing in the background as I wrote that.

What are a few areas in which teenagers need to keep their promises? Maybe a list would help. I'll start you off, but I want you to keep adding to the list at the end.

- Being on time (Sorry, I said it was a peeve.)
- Doing what they say they'll do, like chores.
- Completing homework, on time (ha, again with being on time.)
- Answering text messages from parents, in an agreed upon time frame.
- Being nice to their siblings. (That is a promise they made to you, isn't it?)
- Being nice to their parents. (Definitely a promise.)
- Telling parents of their whereabouts, if agreed upon as a family.
- To *not* leave the family car gas tank on empty after they use it.
- To tell the truth.
- To confide in their parents when they are in trouble or threatened.
- No texting while driving.
- To abstain from sex, drugs, and alcohol until a time that both parents and the teen agrees upon. (A tough one for everyone involved.)
- To abstain from cigarette and e-cig smoking.
- Please add to the list, parents.

Now parents, let's spend some time thinking back when you were teenagers. You didn't always keep your word, did you? Admit it; you didn't, I know. I didn't either. And guess what? Your teens will not always keep theirs. It goes with the age and territory. Once you realize this fact, handling the times they slip up becomes easier. First, decide what on the list is a BIG DEAL to you. Being on time might not make you crazy. (Really? How do you manage that? I want to know.) But non-negotiables will be on the list. Being nice to parents and siblings? Yep, that one's important. Abstaining from alcohol or drugs? Another biggie.

So, pick your battles. If you get outraged at everything, being outraged at your big deals loses impact. Unless your teenager simply doesn't keep his or her word about *anything*, then give them some slack on the lessor missteps. But keep firm hold of the larger digressions and let them know what exactly is unacceptable. Remember, young adults need boundaries, so let them know yours and when they jump the fence, react accordingly. Just don't overreact every time they stray out of bounds. Good luck and God bless—you'll need it on this one!

Parenting Tip

We haven't talked much about "boundaries" yet in this book, and now may be the right time. At some point in the teenage years, usually early on, your children will tell you they no longer need the boundaries you gave them as young ones. Do not, I repeat, do not believe them. Structure will still provide much needed security in their lives, although they rarely will admit it. Undoubtedly, you can relax certain boundaries as they age and as they prove they can be reliable and consistent with the new border. Curfew is the example that can be most flexible. And any boundary that can be relaxed can be restricted again, too. Remember, that's always an option.

You can talk to your kids about boundaries. Tell them exactly what they are and the consequences of breaking them. Set up the rules beforehand. Be sure the consequences are reasonable and enforceable. For example, a missed curfew results in loss of phone privileges for five days. (*Five days!! My life is over, over!)* Then be sure to follow through. As they mature, be sure to pick a boundary to relax—to show your empathy and love for them. And compliment them when they continually meet the standards you've given them—a great self-esteem boost.

Parents Prayer

Good and heavenly Father, help me to keep my word. Banish all deceptions, half-truths, and little white lies from my life. Be my filter as I commit to my family and spouse. Guide me as I set the example of keeping promises and commitments. When I am tempted to over-commit, make me hesitate and reconsider. Thank you, sweet Jesus. Amen.

Stretch the Strategy

1. Do you always tell the truth?
2. What's your personal philosophy about "little white lies"?
3. Do you always keep your promises? Why or why not?

#17
Equip Your Teens to Take Constructive Feedback

Refuse discipline and end up homeless; embrace correction and live an honored life.

—Proverbs 13, *The Message*

---

otice when I titled this chapter I didn't use the phrase "constructive criticism." Let's drop that vernacular from our conversations with kids. After all, if it's criticism, how can it be constructive? Most teens don't like to be criticized. Most *adults* don't like to be criticized either! So, let's strike criticism from the parent/teen vocabulary and go with a much more versatile word—feedback.

The word *feedback* first arrived in our lexicon in the music world. It's the sound that reverberates from the speaker back to the sound system. Remember those loud, screeching sounds, hard on the ears? The Beatles supposedly first used feedback in a creative way in music, recording it onto a record. Listen to the first several notes to the song *I Feel Fine* to hear the feedback. The Fab Four proved feedback didn't always have to be hard on the ears. It can be creative.

So, look for creative ways to deliver constructive feedback.

Please don't wait days to discuss a critical situation. For feedback to be effective, it needs to come quickly—just not loud and screeching. If your teen—or your husband or wife, for that matter—does something that you deem deserves a little feedback, do your best to deliver it almost immediately.

Now, it might work to delay the feedback a few minutes to give yourself some time to think through what you'd like to say, rather than utter the first words that come out of your mouth. Let's designate an arbitrary timeframe, one hour, for instance. Any longer and you or the observed offender may forget about the whole incident. So, if you have to wait longer than an hour to deliver feedback, you may consider letting the whole matter drop. Don't worry, there'll always be more chances with teens needing feedback just around the corner.

It also might work to have a few opening lines ready when you deliver the news. How about one of these?

- Okay, a little feedback here?
- You might consider it this way...
- Hmm, that was an interesting way to handle that. Tell me what you were thinking.

Try to avoid some of the more common openings, like:

- Are you kidding me!? (I've probably used this one before. Okay, I admit it, I have.)
- Oh my God, oh my God!
- What in God's name were you thinking?
- Do you have any idea at all what you just did?
- Do you realize the implications of your actions?
- Just wait till your father (or mother) gets home!
- I have a much better way to handle that.

- Okay, right there, what you just did, that's a teaching moment.
- Let me tell you exactly what you did wrong there, okay? (That's me again...darn.)

Once you deliver the feedback, please get some feedback of your own. Consider these questions to ponder after you deliver:

- Did your child understand what you were trying to say?
- Did the discussion make an impact? (Not all will; remember, pick your battles.)
- Did you deliver the feedback with sincerity and grace? Maybe even a little humor?
- Is your child still smiling?
- Are you still smiling?
- Did the conversation create more tension than it should have?
- Has your child all of a sudden become quiet and defensive??

If you deliver feedback on a regular basis, keep it light and humor-filled, and, if you can, lace it with sincerity and grace, your teenager will begin to accept the feedback. (We can always hope, right?) Maybe he or she will even begin to ask for feedback on certain subjects (like dating, friendships, relationships). Start early in their childhood, don't always deliver feedback as punishment, and as the child grows into the teenage years, accept that their view and your view will differ at times. Acknowledge that the way they handle situations can work, too. Acquiesce some situations—the ones with fewer consequences—to their judgment. Let them learn from their mistakes. You may even learn that their approach is appropriate, too. All of these ideas will help you understand the American teenage mind. Wouldn't that be sweet!

Parenting Tip

Okay, let's get real, parents. For your kids to fully appreciate this strategy, you are going to have to lead by example. Each parent, if there are two in your family, should be prepared to talk about their shortcomings. With very specific examples.

I'll go first. As a young buck working in Silicon Valley, one of my first management jobs was with a company in trouble. They had horrible cash flow problems, and that infiltrated almost every aspect of doing business—from delivering on time to producing good products. And I adopted an attitude of complaint. When I met with a mentor who helped me with job-related issues, he immediately saw through this "victim mentality." And he made a comment I remember thirty-five years later: *Bruce, you can complain about life, or you can make things happen in life. Which are you going to be? A complainer or a doer?* I took that constructive feedback and immediately quit complaining—well, for the most part. That short conversation changed my life. But if I'd been too consumed with myself to listen to his feedback, I might still be a complainer today. (Full disclosure: I can slip into pessimism pretty quickly; it's my nature. Thank God I have a wife who reminds me of this continually, and gently.)

I could also talk about a few other examples of mine that my kids could actually see and experience. My short temper. My critical nature. Stop me, please. Those two less than stellar traits illustrate prime examples where my wife helped me through with loving feedback. And the kids saw the results.

Parents should not be concerned with revealing shortcomings to children. They probably see them anyway. You needn't risk losing your parental authority. You'll come across as only human, like all the rest of us, and more empathetic to any fault your kids may display.

Parents Prayer

Lord, soften my words when I instruct my children. Allow me to teach and train in the most loving way available. Make me hesitate when my anger flares. Teach me your way of discipline, your voice of caring, your instructions of love. Thank you, sweet Jesus. Amen.

Stretch the Strategy

1. How often do you complain? Discuss with your spouse. (Or your kids.)
2. How well do you take constructive feedback?
3. What's one character trait or tendency you'd like to change or alter this year? How will you go about doing that?

#18

Teach Teens to Recognize and Be Willing to Improve Their Shortcomings

---

Become wise by walking with the wise; hang out with fools and watch your life fall to pieces.

—Proverbs 13, *The Message*

We're back to that self-esteem thing again. Don't get me wrong; I'm big on self-esteem, just not too big. I'm a firm believer that teenagers cannot be told that they are always right, that they're perfect. Nobody's perfect. We succeed and grow because we recognize our strengths and we improve our weaknesses.

You should do all that you can to build a teen's self-esteem. And while you're doing that, be sure to point out the areas in personality and output where the teen needs to improve. You can always have them take formal personality tests, like Myers-Briggs. Many are free online. These tests will help define a teen's basic makeup. There's another one called Emotional Intelligence. Do your research and find a test that works well for teens. Talk to your child's guidance counselor—if they have one—or youth pastor for suggestions on how a teen can know themselves better. Don't put all your weight into these tests but use them as a beginning gauge for your teen.

Then add your input, parents, to the teens' strengths and areas for improvement. That's the most important say-so they can receive. Please be truthful, sincere, kind, and graceful about delivering it. I'm sure you will be.

You can begin to evaluate your teen with the following list I've put together. Pick and choose a few of these areas to evaluate. A few, not all! You don't want to hammer your child over the head with all the areas where he or she needs to improve. You want to have more strengths listed than weaknesses, for sure. And take into account the age and maturity level of your child when evaluating.

Leadership Skills

1. Does your child take responsibility for their actions?
2. Do they listen well?
3. Do they make good decisions?
4. Are they coachable and approachable?

Communications Skills

1. Can they get their points across, so they are understandable?
2. Are they open to talking about things?
3. How are their negotiation skills?
4. How are they at receiving feedback? Giving feedback?
5. What do their non-verbal behaviors convey? (Are they the master of the eye roll?)

Team Skills

1. Do they ask good questions?
2. Are they willing to help without being asked?
3. Do they participate with others (family, friends, relatives, teams)?
4. Are they reliable?

Organizational Skills

1. How do they manage their personal time?
2. How is their attention to detail?
3. Do they finish projects and tasks on time? (I know, I know…it's just not me, right?)
4. Do they understand basic financial principles?

Creativity Skills

1. Can they identify problems or concerns?
2. Can they problem solve, either on their own or with help?
3. Can they be inventive?
4. Can they brainstorm?

Interpersonal Skills

1. Do they frequently show empathy?
2. Are they confident?
3. How do they handle stress?
4. Do they have a positive outlook?
5. Can they display enthusiasm?
6. What does their personal appearance convey?
7. What do you observe about their interactions with their peers and adults other than their parents?

As you can see, many categories exist to evaluate, so don't go overboard. I don't think making a chart with all of the categories above with a checkmark either "yes" or "no" in each column is a great way to get your points across. Start slowly. Find one, two, or three areas where your child needs to improve. Help them identify those and come up with ideas to improve in each. Give them feedback and examples. Be sure to point out during the day when they were either improving in the selected area or sloughing off. And go overboard when you see *big* improvement. Encourage, congratulate, and celebrate huge improvements. That way your teenager sees improvement as a good thing, a thing to strive for, and a challenge worth fighting for.

If you want biblical examples of how people in the Bible improved their weaknesses, you won't have to look far. Read stories to your kids about Moses (not me, Lord, not me) or Joshua (I'm scared to death, Lord) or Elijah (take my life, Lord, I'm so discouraged) or Peter (I'm so unworthy, I denied him.) The Bible is chock-full of stories—not of how great men and women did great things for God—but of how ordinary people relied on God to do great things.

I understand not all teens will be leaders, excel in creativity, or be great communicators. Everyone displays special gifts and talents, and nobody is skilled at everything. But the above categories are a good place to start. The questions will help parents and teens identify actions and behaviors and maybe even personality. We all have strengths and we all can improve. Identify strengths in your teen and those strengths will be rock solid over time. Identify a few areas to work on— shortcomings—and with the right guidance, instruction and feedback, your teenager will show signs of improvement. At this point in life, that's about all we can ask for, isn't it? Admit it, you'd be thrilled with that, wouldn't you? Uh huh.

Parenting Tip

Now it's your turn, parents, to be the role model. Again. I know, it's relentless, isn't it? Always being this role model. But, hey, it comes with the job. Take one of the skills sections above—Leadership, Communications, Team, Organizational, Creativity, or Interpersonal—and talk about yourself. You are going to have to be brutally honest, because your teen will know if you're fudging or exaggerating. Your teen probably knows you almost as well as your spouse. Just talk about how you developed a set of skills, how you had to work on certain ones, how you excel in an area (or don't) and how you recognize your need to improve. It'll be a great bonding time with you and your child. They'll learn more about their mom or dad and what they struggle with. They may even show a little empathy for you. And it's a great learning experience. All good things.

Parents Prayer

I want to teach my children well, Lord. Help me to listen to their individual needs and to be aware of their special talents. Instruct me in leadership skills so my children learn to take instruction. Advise me in the ways you listen and teach us. Thank you, sweet Jesus. Amen.

Stretch the Strategy

1. Find a book about creativity that you could read and pass on what you've learned to your child.
2. Pick one area – Leadership, Communications, Team,

Organizational, Creativity, or Interpersonal—that you'd like to improve this year. How would you proceed to improve that skill?

#19
Be the Best Voice in Your Child's Ear

Children are a wonderful gift. They have an extraordinary capacity to see into the heart of things and to expose sham and humbug for what they are.

—Desmond Tutu

Voices bombard your children beginning early in their lives. Voices may come from TV commercials and programs, music, school, friends, friends' parents, the internet, Instagram, Snapchat, Facebook, YouTube, TikTok…it's never-ending and relentless.

If they don't hear your voice in the cacophony of messages—and hear it loud and clear—they may steer off track, swayed by a siren's song or a rebel yell.

So, listen to what your child hears from other voices. Get them to replay those messages back to you. Validate the ones you believe are right and true. Counter those you believe to be false. Like the old saying about computers—garbage in, garbage out—do your best to filter out the garbage that enters into your children's minds.

When my kids were teenagers, they had friends whose parents let the teens drink alcohol in their homes. Their voice said: it's okay if it's in our home. That was unacceptable to us. And we explained to our kids why it was. (I don't have to explain it here, do I?) Maybe I do: one, it's illegal. Two, we didn't know how much they were serving or how they were controlling it. And three, who the heck are they to be serving my kids booze without my consent?

Your teenager becomes especially vulnerable to these messages from others because you are not around them as much as you were when they were younger. And other influential teens who hang with yours begin to develop their own voices, however misled and off course they may be. They begin to spout off vague, weird, and in some cases, harmful expressions of life. They think they know quite a bit; but you and I know they are merely puppy dogs leaping at balls tossed every which way—full of energy and enthusiasm but definitely capable of chaos and, sometimes, utterly uncontrollable.

A relationship with the opposite sex illustrates a prime example. Ask your teens what others are saying about dating. If they are truthful with you—a big stretch, I know because this is difficult to express, especially to parents—you might be shocked at the perception teens have about how to approach a steady relationship.

Here's an even harder subject to approach: pornography. During the teenage years, porn becomes a lure. Some kids investigate; some don't. And some kids get hooked. The messages or voices they hear about porn from friends or the uneducated is that "it's not all that bad" or "what's it hurt?" or "no big deal, don't judge me." But scientific study according to the Reward Foundation and others reveals that porn addictions have drastic consequences. It's been linked to depression and higher drug and alcohol consumption. Porn affects the brain's ability for decision-making, memory storage, and information processing. It negatively shapes romantic relationships, misconstrues how we look at our bodies, and leads boys to believe that sexual harassment is acceptable. Bad stuff all around. Don't just preach to teens that porn is wrong and immoral. Show them the scientific facts—it's just like other addictions—mind-altering, dependency-creating junk.

This is not a book to delve into the depths of pornography. If you believe your child is looking at porn, find ways to extract them from it. Look for resources that give you tactics because it's no different than other addictions. Focus on the Family's website provides many blog posts, books, and other tools; be sure to check it out. Remind your child that Jesus always looks over their shoulder—to protect them, guide them, and yes, assess them. It's not fun—voice of experience writing here—to have Jesus observe you looking at pornography. Do not ignore this because it can steamroll into a lifetime addiction with bad, bad outcomes. Take action, be assertive, love your child enough to help them out of this darkness.

Don't be afraid to challenge what they are learning in school either. Pick up one of their textbooks and read a bit. History texts are often rewritten every generation (or less.) This sells more textbooks and allows for "new thinking" to enter the book. "New thinking" is in quotation marks because "new" does not necessarily mean true or right. Math is another example. First there was "math". Then "new math" and now "new, new math", sometimes exemplified by Common Core. Kids today are taught more about the conceptual understanding rather than memorization. "Whole language" infiltrated English and spelling instruction, teaching meaning and strategy rather than phonics-based methods of reading and writing. Considering how poorly the American teen stacks up against teens in other developed nations, parents need to dig deep to see these changing standards. Sometimes tried and true is better than hip and new.

A good time and place for these conversations used to be at the dinner table, five-thirty p.m. sharp in many households. Maybe six p.m. if Dad got home late. Now I see many families missing this opportunity. Teens are over-committed with after-school activities, younger children demand attention, and both parents may be working. You may find it hard to get all of the family around the dinner table at the same time.

Maybe this task of tackling the tough topics falls to Mom or Dad, designated by a vote of the parents with input from the teen, and a time and place for conversation develops. Saturday mornings going out to breakfast. After dinner in the teen's room, after homework is done. Find a time; make it consistent; have a few things to talk about; just show up and share a little give and take. Most teens will relish more time with Mom and Dad as long as you don't make it a critique session. Don't call their friends wrong or stupid (even if they are); just point out the difference in opinion and why you think the way you do.

Make it fun, light, informative, and easy. This is the time to mesh being a parent with being a friend and confidant. With a boy, a father can speak to relationships and dating girls (with Mom's input) and other topics that may make a boy uneasy to share with Mom. With a girl, Mom is often the most trusted voice in the room (with Dad as a verified consultant, often times in the other room.) Most teens know that they don't know everything and can use another voice to either verify or disregard what they *think* they know.

These conversations will also develop the teen's ability to communicate. You can be too dictatorial, parents, if your approach is always "my way or the highway". This is a two-way, four-lane highway where both sides build their voice. Learn to stretch the teen's thinking—give and take, back and forth—not give, give, give by the parent.

If you, as a parent, are not the best, most consistent, and most caring voice in your teenager's ear, he or she will find one that is. Isn't that a scary thought?

Be the best voice. Be the most caring. And show your teen how much you love them by always being available to listen.

Parenting Tip

Parents, talk about your relationships with the opposite sex when you were a teen. Make sure to include the challenges you faced—and the solutions you've discovered.

Also, talk about the way females and males differ in relationships. Talk about how maturity helps us understand each other; about how we learn from mistakes and misunderstandings; about how as we grow older, we are less apt to base our relationships on what others say or how people look. Talk about communication techniques (like asking open-ended questions) that get the other person to open up. Make this an ongoing conversation, a regular part of what teens and parents talk about, not a special "birds and bees" type exchange.

Parents Prayer

Lord, help me to be your voice with my children. Help me to teach them your love and grace; and to teach them your ways. Curb my negativity, enhance my joy as I talk through tough issues with my family. Always allow your glory to shine through. Thank you, sweet Jesus. Amen.

Stretch the Strategy

1. Talk with your friends, who have children in similar grades as yours, about the textbooks your kids are reading.

2. Do you have a strategy to talk to your kids about "the birds and the bees"?

3. Do more research about the harmful effects of porn.

#20
Train Teens to Protect Themselves Without Seeing the World as a Scary Place

---

I am going to notice the lights of the earth, the sun and the moon and the stars, the lights of our candles as we march, the lights with which spring teases us, the light that is already present.

—Anne Lamott

Life these days can be scary. If you're not a little scared about what is happening all over the globe, maybe you haven't been paying attention. After the Great Recession, the rise of global terrorism, social unrest, and a global pandemic, we face an uncertain future in many regards. Times may get worse before they get better. Solutions to worldwide problems do not appear clear, concise, or in consensus. I hope by the time you read this, COVID-19 and social justice issues are in the rearview mirror, but I doubt it.

Even if we believe with all our hearts that God is good, in charge, and our ultimate victory is guaranteed, we also know we live in a fallen world. Full of bad people with bad intentions.

However, the world has always been a dangerous place. If

you are a Baby Boomer, in your lifetime you have experienced the Vietnam War, the AIDS epidemic, gas shortages, 18 percent interest rates, assassinations, and much more. Millennials can make a similarly sinister list, including jihads and a worldwide recession. Today may seem more extreme than yesteryear, but don't get carried away. It's always tough out there, and you've always had to be careful.

Some teens can be oblivious to what's happening in the world or their neighborhood, much beyond their plans for this weekend. One of your most important jobs is to teach teens to protect themselves. They should know the basics of:

- How to say NO and mean it
- How to disengage approaching trouble
- How to escape an ominous turn of events
- How to recognize potential threats

I'm not talking about the boogeyman, some made-up movie monster under the bed. I'm talking real life trouble. Child molesters. Drug peddlers. Thieves. Sexual predators. Internet vandals. Scam artists.

If you don't talk to your kids about these threats, they will stay naïve, too trusting, juvenile, and clueless. Not a good place to be today. But if you *always* express every fear and become terrified of the outside world yourself, you will turn your children into scaredy-cats and they will shrivel, shake, and shirk in straitjackets of anxiety.

Before high school, my son played basketball on an elite team that traveled throughout California—and sometimes beyond—for tournaments. The lone white player on a team of black kids, he learned immeasurably—about different cultures, music, parenting, money, privilege, and more. (So did his mother and I.) When he joined his all-white high school team and they had to travel to play predominately black squads, most of his teammates became intimidated—or scared. They didn't have the background, the experience, and the exposure to that environment. They even commented to themselves that they lived "in the bubble"—isolated and unaware. They had nothing to be scared about, but that fear still persisted.

You may need to expose your kids to different situations and environments, showing them what *not* to fear. Give them tools to combat this fear but don't neglect to talk about it. Be positive in your approach, and if you think there could be threats that will affect your kids, bring those up and discuss.

Here are some ideas to help:

- Show them how to speak up and have their voice heard without being afraid.
- Instruct them on the best way to confide in teachers, counselors, and confidants, including friends but not limited to them.
- Teach them to trust but not blindly.
- Train them to ask pertinent questions.
- Train them to stay in small crowds of friends, not venturing alone.

Now, for the more immediate, physical dangers they may encounter:

- Help them program 911 into their phones for one-touch help in case of emergencies.
- Provide a siren or shrieking whistle for their keychain.
- Teach them to raise their voice and yell "NO" or "HELP".

You will find resources to help here. Don't shirk this responsibility.

One tool that must be in every parent's toolkit is a book by Opal Singleton, *Seduced, The Grooming of America's Teenagers*. You can begin to get a sense of her work at her website, www.millionkids.org. Please check it out, now. In the book, she paints the world as a very scary place—with predators at every turn. This short, quick-read book will open your eyes. If you think you know the world of digital predators—forget it, you don't. Trust me on this one.

Let me quote a little of her book:

"When you hand a smartphone to a pubescent twelve-year-old, you are opening the door for global input from thousands of people you will never meet. The child will spend more time with their internet friends than they will with you. This will mold their thinking. There is no training tutorial. It is pure trial and error and input from their friends. Most parents are naïve to the dangers of the world of apps, video chat rooms, live streaming and online gaming, and so we have just handed them the keys to a digital vehicle with absolutely no instructions...."[4]

It is a scary world—and teens need to know the dangers. And they need to know that their best resource to fight against the evils in the world is their parents.

Some tips that may guide you in this pursuit:

- Teach them to come to you with fears and express them.
- Teach them that no feelings are inconsequential. If you feel it, it's real.
- Help them learn to confront fears and offer advice to combat them.
- Confide that you have similar fears sometimes and how

---

[4] Opal Singleton, *Seduced*, Exulon Elite, 2015, p. 72.

you deal with them. (Do you?)

- Point out all the support that your child has: parents, siblings, friends, police, and others, too.
- Tell them that you love them.
- Tell them that God loves them.
- Show them how God is in charge.

We all want to raise children that are aware and tuned in to what surrounds them and threatens them. We all want to provide kids with the tools to stay safe. And we all want children that are happy and not full of fear about the world around them. It's a big challenge—but together parents and children can create this balance.

Parenting Tip

Much has been discussed about the "softening" of American kids. Boys are encouraged to get in touch with their "feminine side." Girls are prodded to compete with boys in almost everything, including boxing and football. Ridicule rains down on boys if they don't stand up to bullies. Harassment and exclusion follow girls through school and into the workplace.

Find ways to toughen up your children. Find examples of people who stood up for what they believed. Have your son do this research with your help. You might watch the movie *Braveheart* as an example and talk about what William Wallace sacrificed and why he did it. (Just beware: there's a ton of blood and guts, literally, in that movie.)

Here's an example of how "softness" creeps into our child sports. I coached both my son and daughter in their early years playing soccer. Especially as kids begin that sport, women and men parents both volunteer as coaches. I know this will sound like a generalization, but women coaches tend to baby their boys and girls more than men coaches. In soccer, you get knocked down, sometimes hard enough to cry, especially as six- or seven-year-olds. Women coaches I experienced would run out on the field, scoop up the child, and head to the sidelines. Poor baby. I would walk out, inspect for injury, and ask one questions: "Do you want to stay in the game?" Usually, I would get this response: sniffle, sniffle, yes. Okay, let's continue. Both boys and girls will stop crying and start playing.

You may also try fitness training here. Put your boys (and girls) through rigorous physical challenges. Encourage them to succeed but make the challenges hard enough that failure is a possibility. Congratulate them when they succeed; encourage them to work harder when they do not. This fitness exercise will work for males and females. Just be sure to find ways to make it fun. Nobody should be forced to run a five-minute mile around the high school track.

Then teach your girls to stand up to bullies or to walk away with head held high. Be sure to discuss how biased teachers who think boys are better students in science and math can ignore girls in science class. Those are just several examples. Keep digging and you'll find more.

Parents Prayer

Good, gracious Lord, help me to always listen to the fears of my children. Help me to show them that you are always present, that even when I can't listen, you can. When I can't answer their questions, let me point them to you. May I always encourage them to trust in your sovereignty, your grace, and your love. Thank you, sweet Jesus. Amen.

Stretch the Strategy

1. How do you see the world? Scary? How did your view of the world evolve? How did your parents view the world?
2. What resources are available in your community that can help inform you of the situations locally that you should be aware of?

#21
Always Keep the Channel of Communication Open with Your Teens

---

If our children are going to learn how to determine right from wrong, they must know what truths are absolute and why. They need to know what standards of behavior are right for all people, for all times, for all places.

—Josh McDowell, *Right from Wrong*

As your teenagers gain independence from you as parents—and remember, that's part of growing up and a big part of your job—keeping the lines of communication open can be challenging. As we discussed earlier, other voices and different messages invade their airspace. If you don't keep communicating with them, the vacuum fills with questionable dialogue. Teens more and more listen to peers and ignore parents. (Hmmm…maybe it's always been that way.) In fact, this is a normal developmental characteristic of adolescents.

As life gets more complicated, intense, and realistic, some teens can retreat inwardly to try and figure things out on their own. Boys at this age may have one or two trusted male compadres that will become their primary confidants. Girls may tend to trust groups of girls or "cliques" to decipher the intricacies of teenage life. Even church kids who attend a regular youth group environment will not open up to adults— and especially parents—if intimidated, ignored, or impaired. Let me explain.

When teenagers feel intimidated by their parents, they may see their own ideas as unworthy. Opinions may be suppressed; conversations can by muted or shallow. Teens feel afraid of their parents, so they don't engage as much. They follow the rules, mostly, until the time when they no longer feel the need to follow the rules. Parents, you may or may not notice the change; rule followers simply tell you what you want to hear. That's dangerous because parents can be too busy with jobs, marriages, and other children to dig deeper.

When teens feel ignored by their parents—or the subtler actions like "overlooked" or "discounted"—they lose confidence in their parents to be that best voice in the lives. I know very few parents do this consciously. It simply happens as life becomes overwhelming. Teens can drift away to consume other inputs and may develop judgments against their parents, even subconsciously. Teens simply depend on their parents less and less. Again, that's dangerous on many levels.

When teens feel impaired by their parents, they can feel quality time with mom or dad diminishing—or that the strength or value of the bond between parent and child is decreased. This may happen without a conscious understanding either by the child or the parents. Life takes over; school takes precedent; boy/girl relationships take control. Parents fade into the background. Typical you may say. And yes, it is. But now is not the time to cut back on conversation. It's the time to make a more strategic effort to open the lines of communication.

Try the approach of discussing "big ticket items" with your

teen. These can be discussions about topics that loom large in nature and depth, will affect your teen dramatically in some manner, and may have different layers of understanding for a teen to grasp. For instance:

1. *The Talk*: birds and bees. If you haven't had that talk before the teenage years, you're behind—but it's not too late. The initial conversation could take an hour or two (or a night away from home at a campground or hotel), but the ensuing talks can be almost endless. As you've probably figured out yourselves, parents, the opposite sex is an intriguing, beguiling, and bewildering topic.

2. *Boy/Girl Relationships*. These scenarios are endless. Find a current question or concern from your teen and just talk it out. No judgment, no criticism, no absolutes. "If it were me" is a good lead-in to discussing how a situation may be handled. Relating to similar situations between husband and wife can bring the discussion closer to home and make it believable and real. Even reviewing arguments or miscommunications between parents can open doors for discussion with teens, although it's probably not the preferred circumstance. But it does show that adults struggle and are able to work through problems.

3. *College or life's next step*. College is not for everyone, nor is junior college. But teens are always concerned about what will happen after high school. It's never too early to begin to talk about what will come next. Don't let this conversation slide or slip through the cracks. Don't concentrate on what is expected, what everyone in the family has always done in the past, or what you want, parents. Talk about choices, alternatives, and outcomes. Paint a picture of the future with your teen's input and their passions so they can begin to develop a story in their head of how to achieve a future they want. Not a future you

want for them. Huge distinction. And this topic cries out to takes notes in a notebook, diary, or journal.

4. *Money*. Oh, the possibilities! A never-ending topic full of misconceptions and misnomers. Checkbooks, credit cards, cash, stock market, real estate, savings plans, taxes—oh, the places you can go. Start basic and keep it simple. Don't try to review everything all at once—that would be overwhelming, don't you agree? Find a simple book, if you can, to explain the definitions. Show and tell: your checkbook as a family or your IRA/saving plan/social security statement can open up ideas that can make the discussion both fun and real-life to the teen. Show them your paycheck and discuss the deductions and reductions from what you earn to what you are paid. Be ready for indignation by the teen—then be ready for explanation. Don't gripe and complain about paying taxes or working for "the man"—that will only make a complainer or malcontent out of your child.

Those four topics—sex, relationships, future planning, and money management—provide enough detours and excursions into other related material that keeping the lines of communication open with teenagers will not be a problem. One final reminder: don't go overboard. Keep it light and simple and fun. Teens have enough to worry about, especially in these arenas. Your job as parents is to be the voice of reason, the voice of confidence, the voice of experience. That way your teens will return again and again to hear more. Teens that learn to discuss topics and strategize outcomes become adults who are confident in their ability to solve problems and take action. Let's raise more of those.

Parenting Tip

It's usually a good idea to think before you talk, especially about sensitive topics like the ones we've covered in this chapter. And it's not always possible. Sometimes you have to make a point and make it quickly. Fine, I get that. But it's perfectly fine to "delay" the conversation for a time with your child. If you need more time to think about your response—or to collaborate with your spouse on what you both decide will be the parental consensus—by all means take a short timeout. Don't delay for days or weeks but postpone if you have to. Better a good response than simply a quick one.

Note of Caution: One of my early readers for this book had a serious problem with his teenage daughter and an eating disorder. He and his wife almost missed the signs and only another parent pointing out a serious weight loss for their daughter brought it to light. Even parents with great communication with their children can miss what a teen wants to hide from them. You simply have to be involved, parents. Keep your eyes and ears open. Ask questions. Talk to other parents, too. Girls can slip into trouble easily, with eating disorders, drugs, sex—our daughters are so vulnerable. Boys, too—and throw guns, porn, and violence onto the boy pile. No teen is immune; all are at risk. Please be aware—I'm not trying to scare you. Well, maybe a little. (Because…yes, it is scary, a little, huh?)

Parents Prayer

Thank you, Lord, for my children. They are a gift from you. I'll need your help sometimes to talk with them. Show me ways I can teach them right from wrong, good from bad. Teach me to listen to their voices and to penetrate through the many voices that speak to them. Guide me through those difficult talks, and give me strength to speak your voice, with love and grace. Thank you, sweet Jesus. Amen.

Stretch the Strategy

1.   What topics have been taboo in your family? Why? Can you find a suitable way to broach the topic with your kids?
2.   Are you ever unavailable for your kids? What can you do to remedy that situation?

#22
Do Not Solve Every Problem for Your Teen

I roamed the countryside searching for answers to things I did not understand. Why shells existed on the tops of mountains. Why the thunder lasts a longer time than that which causes it and why immediately on its creation the lightning becomes visible to the eye while thunder requires time to travel. How the various circles of water form around the spot which has been struck by a stone and why a bird sustains itself in the air. These questions and other strange phenomena engaged my thought throughout my life.

—Leonardo da Vinci

Right on the heels of advice to keep the lines of communication open with your teenager comes the counterpoint of resisting the urge to solve every one of their problems. I know, I know, we don't want to see our children in the throes of trouble. It's hard seeing them in a dilemma—one where we can clearly see the best way out—and not tell them exactly what to do. And it's equally as hard to resist correcting every mistake they make, or before they make it, so they don't have to suffer the consequences.

You always want to be a good, sound voice in their ear as much as possible, talking through situations regularly and intimately. But if you tell them exactly what to do for every situation, you grow young adults unable to make decisions and accept outcomes.

As my good friend and fellow author Hal McLean (*The Enduring Organization*) says: *"Do not open the cocoon for them."*

The butterfly needs to struggle to get out of the cocoon to develop their strength to fly. If the cocoon is slit open "to save them" from the struggle, the butterfly is unable to fly and dies. Similarly, parents can resist the urge to intervene and prevent the struggle, at the same time acting as the teen's biggest fan during the struggle.

You can certainly be a sounding board for your teen as they discuss dilemmas. And you can do the same after the fact, when the situation has resolved or the dilemma dissolved. Recap, review, and evaluate—always a good strategy.

God rarely tells us exactly what to do. He may lead us, show faith in us, encourage us and correct us. But he gives us free will. We can always ask him that his will be done in our lives, and the closer we get to him, the better we'll understand his will. But we still do the "doing" part.

In what areas of a teen's life do they need to make their own decisions? I'll offer a few suggestions, but each individual is different. Not all rules will hold true for each teenager. Some kids mature more quickly; others have a greater allotment of common sense or worldliness about them. You are the final judge of how much decision-making and in what arenas they are capable. You obviously don't want them making decisions that will alter their entire lives in one split second. Pick a few of the instances below to begin *to let go and let them.*

1. *Let them choose their own friends.* Relationships come and go throughout junior and senior high school so a bad choice here may be short-lived. Of course, bad choices in friendships can certainly have terrible outcomes (sex, drugs…rock 'n roll. No, scratch that last one!)—and your advice in this arena should be given. But don't demand that friends be discarded; don't declare that they cannot see another person. This may make you appear like a dictator, and your advice might backfire. They may keep those friends simply because you say they can't. If you think your teen is making poor choices when choosing who they hang out with, invite those friends to your home and dig deeper to get to know the people who are influencing your child. Do not, I repeat, do not neglect to know your children's friends. They can have a more influential voice to your child than you do. Find ways to make your home fun for kids to hang out. A swimming pool or ping pong table, video games…something. You want them at your house. You want to get to know them.

2. *Let them spend their money as they choose.* If they run out of money, the outcomes are not devastating at their age. You could bail them out if they're strapped for cash—once or twice. But if you keep doing it, they learn the lesson that Mom and Dad will always bail them out. They will believe Mom and Dad will always be a source of unlimited funds. That doesn't teach independence, it cements dependence. For example, if they spend all their money and don't have enough to buy their lunch at school, going hungry once or twice (or having to beg from friends) is not such a bad way to learn the lesson. If they are out of money by the weekend and all their friends are going for hamburgers and movies, watching reruns of *Seinfeld* with the parental units might cure them of overspending. Oh, the horrors.

3. *Let them date whom they want to date.* Oh, my, did I really write

that? That even scares me. Once you tell them not to date somebody, that exact person seems to be the one they want to date. Funny how that works, isn't it? And frustrating, I know. They will soon find out that relationships with the opposite sex are difficult, and they'll come to realize they want the parent's support and encouragement through the process. And try not to worry; most dating relationships won't last long at this age anyway. A broken heart or crushed ego is a small price to pay and an easy lesson to learn, although the teen may not think that way at the time. Again, if you doubt your teen's choices for dating, get to know that choice. Maybe they aren't so bad; or maybe your teen needs you now more than ever. Don't just take your kid's opinion that the date is super fine. Call up their parents and see if they know their child is on a date with yours. Have a cup of coffee with that mom and see if your values align with hers. Take it a notch or two deeper than you already have.

4. *Let them manage their own time.* Okay, I know we're treading on shaky ground here. Some teens have absolutely no time management abilities—none, zip, zilch. Time runs out before homework is done or chores are completed. Some teens neglect time so that their rest and sleep become negatively affected. But they won't live in your house forever (let's hope, right?), so they need to at least begin to learn time management techniques at this stage of life. Help them when you can; offer suggestions when they struggle. But if you manage all of their time, they will either resent that they have no time for themselves or they will never learn to do it on their own.

5. *Let them create their own "look".* The clothes they wear, the way they style their hair, the makeup they paint on—this is all part of being an individual. Many teens will copy a style they see in others around them. They don't want to look too different—it's safer inside the herd. Others want to rebel and

look completely different (or strange or weird or Goth or whatever.) Don't make such a big deal out of it. Let them experiment. You probably want to draw the line at piercing and inking until a certain age, but that's your call. A bad haircut grows out; a poor choice of clothing for a school picture fades from memory after a few years; a bad dye job for hair eventually rinses away. Appearance is one of the few arenas that belong to each individual teen; don't be too quick to take that away from them.

Your role in this as parents—to let go and let them—prepares the teen for adult life. Give some latitude, offer as few suggestions as needed, be sympathetic for their missteps, and help them recover whenever necessary. Just don't solve every problem and dilemma for them. And hey, you may find out there is a bit less drama circling the homestead if you keep your nose out of each and every teen angst. Wouldn't that be a nice breath of fresh air?

Parenting Tip

Share with your children the circumstances in your life when you had to make a tough choice. Maybe a new job, a financial decision, or a work-related dilemma. Explain your reasoning—and the outcome. Share experiences that both worked out well and some that may not have. Show your child how even decisions that don't work out so well at least achieve action (as opposed to inaction), move yourself forward (instead of standing still), and how decisions build character and confidence.

Parents Prayer

Sometimes, Lord, I don't know why and when to 'let go and let you'. I want to control everything in my life and in the lives of my kids. Help me to learn to trust you, Father. Give me ways that I can instill that trust in my children. Watch over my family when I can't be with them. Protect them—put your heavenly beam of protection over them at all times. Keep temptation and evil away. Thank you, sweet Jesus. Amen.

Stretch the Strategy

1. Do you want to "pave the way for the child" or "prepare the child for the way"? Can you see the distinction? Discuss with your spouse.

2. How much do you trust God? What would help you build more trust in him?

#23
Help Your Teens Explore and Discover Their Passions in Life

Each of us has certain strengths. We were born with them, they will always be our strengths, and we delight in them. Work happens best when we discover these strengths, put them to use, and focus on developing them. Trying to improve our weaknesses is like trying to teach a rabbit to swim or a snail to race.

—John Ortberg, *The Me I Want to Be*

Many teens love to display a nonchalant attitude. They love to be "cool" and unaffected by life's curveballs. It's mostly an act. Believe me, as a teen, I had this one down cold.

Lots of areas of life confuse and confound—and maybe even excite—teenagers, but to admit that would not be cool. So, they downplay and ignore much so they don't have to admit they don't know. We all did it—hid our feelings, stuffed them down inside. That's not always a terrible thing to do, just reactionary and somewhat predictable for that age group. But life doesn't always work too well when we react with nonchalance because it often comes across as uncaring or disinterested.

We might want to shake the teen tree and get some branches moving. As parents we can teach teens to find a passion and express it. Run with it! Shout about it from the treetops! Okay, maybe I went too far—but engaging in excitement and passion is a very, very good thing. It gets the juices flowing, the blood moving (or even boiling), gets you up in the morning, and keeps you stirred throughout the day.

Face it: school and studying will rarely induce that excitement. Did it for you? Yeah, me neither. I secretly envied the kids in my school who really enjoyed school.

Without much intervention and with little prodding from parents, some teens get excited about sports. Others find passion in the arts—music, singing, dancing, or theater. A few even find commitment in study—it fuels them toward college, career, and a calling.

And some teens sit on the couch watching TV or stay in their rooms playing video games. All without purpose or passion. Maybe it's time to ignite the flame.

Parents too detached from their teenager's life struggle to help. Parents that cannot find their own passion might be too frustrated to contribute much. Parents committed to building and growing a life for their teen, setting those youngsters up for success, and launching the teen into the future, tackle this situation with gusto.

Let's discuss a few ideas to move the teen spirit.

- *Expose them to everything you can.* Let diversity be your guide. If they love sports, certainly go to sporting events. But expand their horizons by including live theater, too. Or the zoo. Or stock car races. Or classical music. If they aren't too excited about traveling with the family, make them travel with the family. And mix it up. One time go camping; next time stay in a hotel. See nature in the woods or national parks; see the big city, too. If they don't want to go, make them go. You can always find a compromise. *If you go with us on this trip, we'll do something on the trip that interests you.* You'll be surprised how often they will enjoy the unexpected experience. If as parents, you have limited means and time, concentrate in your city—find ways to expose your teen to different experiences close to home.

- *Show passion in your own life.* Parents can expose kids to their own passion to ignite passion in their children. If your passion is history, show your kids why history is so important to you. If you get riled up about politics, discuss why. Show your passion and even your prejudice if you must, just make it relative to teenagers. Describe times in your past when politics dictated policy—and how the laws reflect that. Civil rights would be a great place to start. If you love country music and your child only loves rap, better take them to see a country band of your choice. (Of course, you may have to compromise and see rap firsthand. I never said this would be easy. I just said it was essential.) If you love baseball and your daughter loves Broadway, take in a game and a play. You'll both be better off for it. If you find passion in feeding the starving children in the world, take your kids to see the horrible reality of starvation and malnutrition. Your children will never be passionate about all things in which you are. That's not the point. The point is to show them how passion lives in your life, how it comes alive, and how it compels you to act.

- *Talk about passion.* Showing and exposing passion is great; now sit down and talk it out. Once teens figure out what their strengths are in life, you as parents can help them to use those gifts and talents. A strength in the written word opens doors to reporting, marketing, public relations, and much more. A talent in math can lead to engineering, astronomy, teaching, and the list goes on. A gift of compassion could result in a life in the world of medicine, nonprofit, or other caring professions. Open these doors for teens who have never seen the other side. If they have discretion in school research papers, have them study these areas that show glimpses of strengths or vitality in their future.

- *Introduce them to professionals in careers that may interest them.* Please don't use this idea as pressure to choose a career at such an early age, just as food for thought and study. Make sure the professional doesn't pitch their career too hard, just answers questions and shows pluses and minuses of the job. Train your teen to ask questions and show appreciation for time and conversation. Don't push your child to replicate your profession; nudge them to discover one that they can become passionate about.

Prodigies happen every once in a generation or a lifetime. A Beethoven may only be born once a century. Passion in life is cultivated, like a field in anticipation of harvest. You must prepare the land. Find the right seed to plant. Care for its growth and maturity. Skillfully plan for the harvest. It doesn't happen overnight or without your input, guidance, and zest, parents. Prepare now for your child to seize their own passion in life. To grab it and hold on. To never let go even when all indicators point to an alternative. To live a life with passion is to feel complete, to feel you were placed on this planet for a purpose, and that you are fulfilling that purpose. To touch God's plan for your life and how it intersects with the universe. To boldly go down your own path, the one especially carved out and prepared for you.

To live a life of self-confidence and responsibility, find your passion.

Parenting Tip

This exercise may take some research, parents. I'd like you to find young people—in the news, in sports, in music, in science—that have excelled at an early age. Not as a way to compare them to your child, but to show that passion—when recognized and channeled—can produce excellence. You might even want to assign this to your teen. Let them do the research. You provide the description, for example: "I want you to find a teenager that has produced remarkable results in science. Go, research!" They will find young boys and girls that have started companies in technology while still in their teens or kids who helped discover new planets or stars. Your job then as parents is to find the reason these kids excelled. Sure, it may be because they are gifted intellectually. But find the spark, the passion, that set them on their course. Look for their tenacity, dig deep to find what makes them tick. At the base, at their foundation, you'll discover this thing called PASSION. It's the igniter. If you can help instill the possibility of your teen finding their passion, look out world. You just may create a child who is full of life, full of learning, full of achievement. Fulfilled!

Parents Prayer

Dear Lord, help me to open up my view of your world. Guide me to explore new possibilities for my children. Speak to us so we hear your voice for our future. Quiet our dialogue as we listen for your vision, your heart, and your calling for us. Thank you, sweet Jesus. Amen.

Stretch the Strategy

1. What are your passions in life, parents?
2. Do you ever read biographies? (Biographies provide glimpses of people finding and using their life's passions.) Find a couple and discuss with your kids.

#24
Let Teens Dream, Dream Big, and Explore

Then the Lord took Abraham outside and said, "Look at the sky, and see if you can count the stars. That's how many descendants you will have.

—Genesis 15:5, CEV

Dreamers get a bad rap these days. To be called a dreamer means your head is in the clouds, that you don't live in reality, that you lose focus or clarity, or that you're not living in the here and now. But I say, fuhgeddaboudit, go on and dream.

If Steve Jobs and Steve Wozniack hadn't dreamed up Apple, we may still be using punch cards in our computers. If Henry Ford, David Dunbar Buick, or the Dodge brothers didn't dream cars and engines and transportation, where would we be? We need dreamers in the world. And we need to dream as teenagers to look for possibilities in the future.

Too many times in life we can only see what's right in front of us. We labor along, nose to the grindstone, neurons in our brains on hold. Teens are notorious for not looking to the future, unless of course, it's this coming weekend. That's about as far ahead as many of them look.

But the teen years are made for exploration. The teen mind needs nourishment to grow, and nothing nourishes like looking toward the future—its hopes, possibilities, and its dreams.

The teen years are not a phase that somehow we manage just to "get through". Okay, I'll admit, there are times that it certainly *feels* that way. Maybe even many times. But rather God designed this time to be an important development stage in life. To grow a young brain and make it expand a bit. The teen years become a time for:

- Developing an emotional spark
- Social engagement
- Novelty seeking
- Creative exploration

It's not a time to sit around and play video games. It's not a time to spend on and in the phone.

Help your teen develop an emotional spark. In Chapter #23, I talked about passion. Parents can help spark that passion. Sparks that ignite in the teen years may not last a lifetime, but they start the process. A teenage brain can be trained to seek the spark; they can learn the process of spark chasing and dream weaving. Teenagers have an innate need to seek out, to explore—it's part of their teenage DNA. Help them seek the spark; never douse the ember that may lead to passion.

When I look back at my high school yearbook and gaze at the activities listed under my name, I still find importance in them. Many pursuits I discovered during my teen years are the activities that keep me passionate today. Yes, they've morphed over the years, but the passions—sports and physical fitness, writing and reporting, leadership—still engage, inspire, and thrill me 40 years later.

Help your teen engage socially. Find ways to get them involved—with other teens and adults. Help them to develop their social skills—their voice, their manners, the connection to others, their listening, and their interaction. I don't mean through social media on their phone or their computer. Encourage them to join a club (you can say it'll look good on their transcript, if you need to.) Find ways they can be part of a team. It doesn't have to be an athletic team; any team will do. Host small groups of their friends at your house. Get to know your child's friends so you can help wade through the waters of crazy teen relationships as a rudder for your teen's ship.

It's also a time for novelty. Teens do wild things sometimes—things that seem a little crazy to adults. But it's not necessarily crazy to them. It's new and different—a novelty. Most aren't harmful; some are, of course and you want to steer them away. But a teen is probably going to smoke a cigarette once in his or her life and if it's one or two, it's not going to kill them. They'll experiment with other things, too, like alcohol. If you make a huge deal out of it, ground them for life for taking a sip, they may gulp down more just to spite you. Sure, tell them it's not good for young brains (or any brains really) and never serve alcohol to their friends (what are you crazy, too?) But let them taste the champagne at the wedding or anniversary. They are going to try it anyway. With marijuana legal in many states and readily available in most, teens may experiment here, too. After all, you probably did, didn't you, parents? I did—and I inhaled, too. Of course, you can be educating them on the hazards of any tobacco use, including the wacky kind.

Don't discourage experimentation or exploration, guide it. The teen mind is a wonderful thing to shape. Eager, energetic, experimental, and easily moldable. Better that you help get the mind into ship shape rather than let it slip away, sulk, or atrophy. Don't you want to raise a child that isn't afraid of new things? Don't you want a child that embraces the unknown and steps up to the challenge of discovery? Wouldn't you rather have a child whose eyes light up at the possibility of change instead of one who shies away from anything out of their comfort zone?

Encourage dreaming. Tell your teen they determine their own destiny, and the only limitation is their inability to dream it and make it come true. I know, I know, you don't want to get their hopes up, paint an unrealistic picture, and have them be disappointed. But who knows? You could be raising the doctor who discovers a cure for diabetes, or cancer, or MS. Lurking in your home could be the social worker that solves the homeless situation in your hometown. That mopey, sullen teen sleeping in your son or daughter's room could be the next big comedian that touches the world's funny bone. Or writes the play that changes the nation's attitude toward race, or women, or gays. Your child could be the worker that is willing to rush back into the office complex to save a life during a firestorm because he or she is not intimidated by fear, the unknown, or the future.

When you raise teens that can dream about the future and anticipate success, they won't get stymied by a setback. They'll have the confidence to dream again.

Let them dream big. If you can't dream big with them, don't squash their dreams. Hey, you might just learn to dream a little yourself. To change your life, your future. It can happen. Trust me, it can.

Parenting Tip

In my preteen years, my grandparents bought me an artist's

easel and paints. I'm pretty sure they were watercolors. I still have a framed photo somewhere of me, in my cowboy shirt, at the easel. Please understand, I have absolutely zero artistic talent in painting. I can't even draw stick figures. But that's not the point. It's experimentation, it's exploring. Those same grandparents also gave me piano lessons. My grandmother could play piano by ear and read music. She tried her darnedest to teach me that skill, too. We would sit at her piano, she'd pick out a lively little number from the sheet music she stored in the piano bench, start tinkling the keys, and I would sit alongside her and mumble the words. It's a very fond remembrance for me. But alas, my music ability went about as far as my painting prowess. Nowhere. Can't carry a tune in a bucket.

Again, not the point. The more preteens and teens experiment and explore, the more they not only learn, but the more they appreciate the process. Developing an appreciation for an area of interest is just as valuable in life. Of course, they'll also learn what they don't like, and that's a good lesson, too. It can be intimidating to try new things, but if you don't try—even if you fail as I did—you'll may never know where your true skills lurk.

Parents Prayer

Show me the dreams that you have for me, God. Open your world up to me and guide me in my path for your goodness. Help me to allow my children to dream their own dreams, unencumbered by my expectations or demands. Show me your way for my kids for your glory. Thank you, sweet Jesus. Amen.

Stretch the Strategy

1. Are you able to dream about your future? Why or why not?
2. Do you have a mind and demeanor that likes to explore? If not, how could you expand this ability?
3. If you don't have the money for art or music lessons, how can you let your child experiment with new skills? Brainstorm ideas.

#25
Say YES More Than NO, but Say NO Often

A 'No' uttered from the deepest conviction is better than a 'Yes' merely uttered to please, or worse, to avoid trouble.

—Mahatma Gandhi

Just so we are clear, I am not in favor of parents being their teen's best friends. You are parents, first, foremost, and always. You can certainly cultivate qualities of friendship and we've discussed several so far. Laughing, listening, being a good voice, dreaming—all great ways friends relate to each other. Fine, I'm all for that.

Please don't view saying yes more than no to their requests as an act of friendship. See that action as a way to display kindness and confidence and trust. Your teen does consider you kind, don't they? Caring and empathetic? I hope you instill confidence and trust in your kids.

If kids only hear NO from parents, they can become discouraged. They could lose the connection to their parents. Remember, they want to explore and experiment. It's how they grow and mature. If all they ever hear is NO, they can become sullen and depressed. We have too many of those American teens already; we don't need more. Or they will turn to their friends as sole confidants. Friends say yes—*sure, let's try it*—and they want to hear yes, so that's where they'll go to hear it.

So, say yes more than no. Let's begin a list of those areas where you can say YES:

1. *Hairstyle.* Don't worry, it grows back. It a personal statement of individuality. What could it hurt, really? Lighten up.
2. *Hair color.* Let their freak flag fly.
3. *Dancing.* Who doesn't love to dance? Teens do. Did you ever see the movie *Footloose*? (I mean the one with Kevin Bacon.)
4. *Dating.* We all want to pick the perfect date for our kids. If only. Might as well say yes, invite the date to your home and get to know them. Then you have a better way of evaluating the choice and discussing it with your child.
5. *Movie choices.* With all the choices of movies online, does it really make sense to say no to, let's say, an R-rated movie? Teens have so many ways to see movies now, you really don't have much control. Go ahead and voice your displeasure with R-rated flicks but say yes to the ones that don't seem over the top.
6. *Having friends over.* Oh, yes! You *want* friends at your house. That way you know what they're doing—and sometimes what they're talking and thinking about. Find reasons to have your child's friends at your home. Buy a Ping-Pong table, convert the garage to a space to hang out, provide the pizza—anything to make it fun to be at your house.
7. *Going away with other families.* You want your teens traveling with other families. That way they won't travel with yours. (No, I'm kidding.) Being with other families makes them be on their best behavior and gives you an excuse to review proper behavior. Plus, they'll come back with new ideas, new foods

they tried, and new conversations they participated in. They'll find new ways to experiment and explore.

8. *Shop for gifts.* If you let your children shop for gifts for others, they learn that skill. Sure, they may mess up once or twice, but they'll learn how to please other people, like their siblings. And we want that, don't we?

9. *Makeup.* Find the right age and tell your female teen that she can start to wear a little makeup then. I'm not the one to determine the age—you are. Teach them how to wear it, what works and what doesn't, and what is too much. If you don't, they'll learn those things from their friends. That's not necessarily a good alternative.

10. *Independence.* You choose the area of independence and monitor the progress. You can always pull it back if the child overreaches or overindulges. But as I've said before, teens have to learn to do things for themselves or they won't learn at all. Driving a car is a big test of independence. How do they use or abuse that privilege? (By the way, teach them to change a tire, too. That'll come in handy for sure.)

I suppose we should list a few things to say NO to, shouldn't we?

1. *Unsupervised excursions before the age of _____.* (You fill in the blank, the age.) Maybe going to the mall with friends before they are, let's say, thirteen, provides too many temptations.

2. *Drinking alcohol.* When you're not present, parents, the legal drinking age is twenty-one. Yeah, I know, they'll do it anyway, but you might as well lay down the law, literally, on this one. If you are present and you choose to let them have a glass of champagne on New Year's Eve, that's your call. But please, do not host parties for your teens and serve alcohol. I needed to say that again because I've seen it done so often—with horrible

results. After all, it is illegal and a huge liability risk for parents.

3. *Illegal drugs.* Anytime.

4. *Prescription drugs obtained illegally.* Anytime, anywhere.

5. *Body piercings.* Okay, maybe ear piercings are fine for young ladies and even nowadays for young gentlemen. But for other piercings, I'd draw the line at age eighteen—but again, that's your call. That's the age when they become legal adults and they can, legally, do what they want and are held responsible for their actions.

6. *Body ink.* Again, if it were me, I'd say have them abstain until the age of eighteen. You could approach it this way: Say yes to tats when they're eighteen. You aren't saying no, you're just saying wait. Might be worth a try. (Oh, I almost forgot, make them pay for it, too.)

7. *Premarital sex.* Until the age of…forty! No, no, just joking. You want to talk openly and honestly about sex—the problems that arise, the risks they take. The "just say no" approach has been proven mostly ineffective—either with drugs or sex. So, take another course. If you had premarital sex, tell them why now you regret it. (You do, don't you?) Don't tell them about the horrors of teenage pregnancy, just the realities—lives changed, opportunities lost, dreams foregone. Do not, I repeat, do not miss the opening to engage teens deeply in this conversation. Do not gloss over it. Do not neglect it. Do your research; know your facts. Sexual tendencies of teens change. Teen pregnancies in the new millennium are down, for instance. But considering what President Clinton engaged in with Miss Lewinsky, guess what sexual activity dramatically increased among teens? Uh, huh. It's a huge problem now. Understand the temptation will always be there. You should be the expert in this discussion because you know your teen hasn't a clue about the subject. Even young Christian couples who are committed to each other are questioning why they shouldn't

have sex before marriage. ("We are planning to marry, so why wait?") Be ready to discuss; show them the Bible verses that prohibit; teach them the sanctity of marriage.

So, I came up with ten things to say yes to and seven to say no to. That's a pretty good ratio. More YES than NO but still some NO. I like that. Let's repeat it.

More YES than NO but still some NO

Let me illustrate one more huge benefit for saying yes, for both the teen and the parent. If they see and hear you saying yes, they can begin to see themselves as people who say "YES"! Why is that important? Because saying yes in life opens doors. It trains us to see an open door as an opportunity, a possibility, an opening to new horizons. If we hear no most of the time, the proverbial door looks closed. Locked even. We want to raise young adults who hear yes, say yes, and respond to yes. We want young adults who see the possibilities in life and grab them. To make their own life. To create their own future. To build a better future—nicer and more open and more friendly and decent. We all want that, don't we?

Yes!

Parenting Tip

The world is not as black and white as it used to be. Yes, we circled back to the "right and wrong" conversation. Relative thinking crept into our society. A sense of right and wrong has been blurred. Your child may say things like: "I can see where you wouldn't do that, but that's the world you live in. What's wrong to you may not be wrong to me."

This is dangerous thinking for young adults learning the difference between right and wrong. Find examples of black and white decisions. (Politics, for example, will never be a black and white discussion. Lying, stealing, killing – those can be black and white, right and wrong discussions.)

Build a sense of right and wrong for your children. Show them your thinking and the standards you use to base your decisions. And read up on the topic of right and wrong. Josh McDowell and Bob Hostetler wrote a great book titled *Right from Wrong: What You Need to Know to Help Youth Make Right Choices.* You may be surprised at how difficult it is for kids, especially today's American teens, to tell right from wrong!

Parents Prayer

Help me to be strong in word and conviction, Lord. Help me to see through deception. Guide me in the long view of discipline and love and help me let go of pleasing my children. I want to be the best parent I can, Father—give me the strength and dedication for my children's future. Thank you, sweet Jesus. Amen.

Stretch the Strategy

1.   Make a list with your spouse of areas in your family to say YES and areas to say NO.
2.   How did your parents influence your opinions on premarital sex and alcohol consumption?

#26
Train Your Teens Not to
Sweat the Small Stuff

*Man is ultimately self-determining. What he
becomes—with the limits of endowment and
environment—he has made out of himself.*

—Viktor Frankel, *Man's Search for
Meaning*

This strategy beckons us all. I snuck this in; it's not just
for teens. Richard Carlson made a boatload of money
writing all those books about not sweating the small
stuff. Why? Because so many of us do. We wanted to find out
how to stop that behavior in those books. Viktor Frankel spent
three years during World War II in concentration camps as a
prisoner. Those that survived often had an outlook of life that
didn't pull them down, didn't let them worry about the small
details.

I think we learn to worry. I don't think we are born
worrying about all the little things that could go wrong. Sure,
some of us see the glass half empty; some actually see the glass
half empty and leaking. (Okay, okay, I admit it, that's me
sometimes.)

But most teens don't. Many live in the here and now and don't develop habits of worry until later in life. Of course, I could make the case that just as many teens are anxious and worry about things to an extreme. It's often times the parents who infuse their children with nit-picky rules, regulations, and regimens. Most teens simply want to get on with life, have some fun while doing it, and explore new and interesting things. Of course, too much fun and exploration can lead to trouble, no doubt about it. I think parents—for the most part, not all the time—could back off all the details about every little thing and let teens take more responsibility for their lives. A constant barrage of clean your room, finish your chores, and get your homework done becomes exactly that—a constant barrage.

Here's an idea: pick a Saturday, declare that all chores, cleaning and homework have the day off and go explore something new as a family. What a fun idea. It doesn't have to cost money, and it will pay dividends.

- A new theme park
- A new movie
- A new miniature golf course
- A new shopping area or mall
- A new hike
- A new place to swim
- A new place to toss a Frisbee or play catch or have a picnic

Get the idea? It might take some work on the parent's part to come up with ideas, but if you include your children and let them participate in the choice—and even invite a friend to go along—most of your work will be done for you.

If parents don't harp on small stuff, kids will still learn that small stuff needs to get done and that it will get done in due time. Again, from Wayne Dyer, "A child who is taught to simply feel guilty or to worry a great deal, is a child who is learning not to take responsibility for changing, but only for feeling bad and helping other to do the same."[5]

You might start by making a list of the small stuff around your household that can take a day off. Things that don't have to get done—by today or even tomorrow.

1. Household chores
2. Cleaning the toilets or cleaning ___ (You fill in the blank.)
3. Paying bills
4. Mowing yards
5. Raking leaves
6. Dusting
7. Laundry; folding laundry.
8. Parents, create your own list from here

Don't sweat the small stuff. If you do, buy the books and do your best to break this habit. Life is too short and there is too much else to teach your teens for you to get trapped in all the details. Keep in mind, I didn't give you a book that outlined the *"85 Strategies to Teach Teenagers Self-Reliance, Confidence and Responsibility."* No, I kept it to 33. I could have added a whole bunch of smaller ones, but I didn't. I wanted you as parents and your teens to get on with life.

Life can be exhilarating. Life with passion accelerates to hyper-exhilarating. But life sweating the small stuff stumbles

---

[5] Dr. Wayne W. Dyer, *What do you Really Want for Your Children?*, Wm. Morrow and Company, Inc., New York, 1985, p. 169.

toward burdensome and depressing. Go for the exhilaration and let go of the burdensome.

Parenting Tip

Almost every young adult will be intimidated by something. Find out what intimidates your child—then work on techniques to overcome the intimidation. This does not have to be accomplished all at one time. Some techniques may work; some may not. Make this an integral part of your mentoring. Keep coming back to this discussion. If your child overcomes one intimidation, work to find another—and another. Here are some examples of what might be intimidating:

- Expressing yourself
- Dating
- Talking to the opposite sex
- Speaking up in class
- Voicing an opinion
- Trying new things
- Talking to adults
- Talking to teachers

Do you know if your teen is intimidated with these circumstances? It may take quiet, one-on-one talks with them to discover the situations that can be scary. Start early because the list will constantly shift as the teen matures. In the midst of tackling these bigger issues, the small details may fade away or seem less stressful. Yeah!

Parents Prayer

Let me learn to trust you, heavenly Father. You say you love me and will always take care of me. Help me to rely on you. I pray that the small details in my life and the life of my children fade away, that you keep me focused on things that matter, and that you give me an attitude of hope. Thank you, sweet Jesus. Amen.

Stretch the Strategy

1. What intimidates you? Discuss with your spouse.
2. What small stuff do you stress about?
3. What big stuff do you stress about?
4. What constructive techniques do you use to relieve stress?
5. How does God enter into this discussion?

#27

Teach Your Teens How to Accept and Embrace Change

A ship in port is safe, but that's not what ships are built for.

—Grace Hopper, inventor

This instruction may be harder for you than for your teenager. Teens can often be taught to embrace changes in life easier than parents who have been set in their ways for years. First, evaluate yourself, Mom and Dad. Do you accept change? Are you at least open for something new and different? A new home, a new job, a new town, even a new career? Those are all huge changes, and many of us struggle with the adjustment, despite the fact that we know the final outcome may be better for us.

Now consider a teen's life. To quote a popular Bob Dylan song, "the times they are a-changin'." (Okay, popular way back when.)

Most everything in a teen's life involves change, like:

- The transition from middle school to junior high or high school.

- The transition through puberty, including changes in the body.
- The development of the brain.
- As schools and neighborhoods change, friends come and go.
- Subjects and teachers in school change constantly.
- Boy/girl relationships change almost weekly it seems.
- Interests change as kids progress through teen years.

But teens may only look at these changes in life…as life. They may not realize that change is happening, and that changes are inevitable in life. Help them realize those reflections, parents. A few suggestions how:

1. *Compliment them on accepting a change.* When changes happen, like from the list above, tell them how proud you are of them for "going with the flow." It helps them decipher what's going on and the progress they're making.

2. *Discuss changes that are hard for you to embrace.* If you've recently changed jobs or responsibilities at work, tell them the difficulties you're having making the transition and how you're handling—even embracing—the change. That prepares them to expect change and have strategies in place to remedy difficulties.

3. *Talk about relationship changes.* Family dynamics can prove fertile ground to discuss how relationships come and go, ebb and wane. A disagreement with a distant uncle or cousin may be treated differently compared to a "heated discussion" with a spouse. The former may have much less impact on the family than the latter. Reviewing your friendships, like discussing old friends you rarely see now, can prepare teens to expect how those relationships will change.

4. *Make a change in your life and embrace it.* Oh, how do I do that, you ask? Mom: change your hairstyle or color, maybe drastically. Dad: shave your beard or grow one. Change where you vacation: Don't go to the same place this year. Always go to the lake? Go to the ocean. Always go camping? Find a nice hotel. Never vacation? Vacation! And make it fun.

5. *Don't make change a big deal.* It's okay to celebrate a job change or a milestone birthday or any number of big changes in your life, parents. Just don't go overboard. Make change routine not overly special.

I changed jobs several times when our kids were growing up. I changed careers and started my own company, too. And I probably suffered through those changes only confiding with my wife about the stresses and the enthusiasm. My kids saw my life changing, but I didn't do enough to explain to them what I was experiencing so they could learn from it. Opportunity missed.

There is an old saying that goes something like this: if you're not changing, you're standing still, going backward, or dying. That's pretty drastic, but the point is life will be full of changes, all the time. The way you view changes shapes your attitude toward life. Resist them and life becomes a struggle. Embrace them and life becomes an adventure. Embrace life changes—and teach your children that skill, too.

Parenting Tip

This one is for Mom. Get a new hairstyle. Admit it, you've wanted one for a while now, haven't you? Maybe you've even discussed it with your daughter. What better time than now to embrace the change! Ooh, how about highlights or lowlights?

(Whatever lowlights are; I know very little about women's hairstyles.)

Okay, the dads are feeling left out. Shave your beard or grow one. Not bold enough for you? Get a new hairstyle. One that isn't from 1985. Or use a little "product" in your hair every once in a while.

Embrace the change! Show your kids you aren't old fuddy-duddies, stuck in the mud! Go, go. Do it now!

Parents Prayer

Open my mind, Father, to see new possibilities in this world. Help me to throw off archaic and out-of-date methods and embrace change. I want to continue to grow and flourish as you give me new ways to think and act, and especially, serve. Thank you, sweet Jesus. Amen.

Stretch the Strategy

1. How did your parents handle change? What did you learn from them about life changes?
2. When you were younger, high school, college or young adult, how did you view change?
3. Has anything changed in the way you view change?
4. Compare notes with your spouse about how you each view change.

#28
Show Your Teens How to Find the Positive in Every Situation

Don't magnify your problems. Magnify your God. The bigger we make God, the smaller our problems become.

—Joel Osteen

One of the most powerful skills you can teach your children—and you must begin even before they reach the teenage years—is to concentrate on the positive. I believe God originally designed us to slant toward the positive, the good, the serene. We didn't inherit a negative demeanor, a defeatist attitude, or depression. Sure, some of us lean more in that direction. And I don't mean to diminish those that are diagnosed as clinically depressed. You came to this world with innate ingredients like compassion, love, empathy, care, giving and other traits of goodness. That's the way God built you. Without getting all gushy-mushy about it, you were made to love. Not hate or dread or despise like we see so much of in America today.

But life intrudes and the impact can be tough, sometimes even brutal. It's not always easy to look on the bright side, is it?

It's not always possible to find the rainbow during the storm. To see the light in the dark. But it is achievable. You have to train your mind, your thinking, to seek and search for the high point, the high ground, the good and clean and fresh and new.

As parents your child will pick up your attitudes and demeanors. They see you display it, and then they copy it. Remember back when they were little toddlers; remember how they mimicked you as they developed their own character? Your speech patterns, your dance moves, your laugh. (Luckily, my kids quickly developed their own dances moves because mine are so pathetic.)

The first step to teach them how to find a positive in every situation is for you as parents to model the behavior. (I know, I know, you thought this book was about how to raise teens to be confident and self-reliable, not how to raise parents for the same purpose. Sorry, maybe I should have put that into the title.)

Let's list a few techniques that work to keep anybody, especially teens, thinking about the positive.

1.   *Take some deep breaths.* It's always crucial to keep breathing. In times of stress, we often actually have to tell ourselves to breath. Go a bit further. Take several very deep, fill-your-diaphragm-and-lungs deep breaths. Inhale slowly, hold a few seconds, and release slowly. Don't pooh-pooh this idea and don't think too much about it. Deep breathing gets the body back in rhythm, fills you with oxygen, and makes you think about something other than your problems. A yoga exercise for increasing the "breath" is to inhale for four counts, hold your breath for four counts and exhale for four counts. Repeat for five and then for six counts. This encourages the deep breathing I'm describing and tends to lower heart rate and blood pressure.

2. *Count to ten.* Slowly, not rapid fire. It's an oldie but a goodie trick. This one slows you down, takes your mind off the situation, increases your breathing, and lowers your heart rate.

3. *Reverse your thinking.* If you think bad, then shift to good. If you think it won't happen, then think it will. If you think about failure, then think about success. When you find yourself or your teen lounging around in the soup of the negative, practice shifting to the complete opposite. Black, shift to white. Ill, shift to healthy. Weak, shift to strong. Bleak, then shift to possible. Whatever the situation, it can always be viewed from the opposite direction. "This will probably never happen" can shift to "this just might happen." Take note of how often your teen describes a situation in the negative or the impossible or the improbable. Help them to shift to the positive, the possible, the likely. It's a subtle change and a dramatic shift in outlook.

4. *Make a list of all the ways to shift the situation.* If your teen has a hurdle to jump over, a situation that looks rather impossible or just plain hard, then make a list of everything that he or she can do to turn it around. Say for instance, they have a big project in school, and they are becoming overwhelmed with completing it on time and done well. Remember back to a time in your life, parents, when big projects seemed daunting. (Maybe they still do....) Most people just need to start somewhere and keep working. Big projects turn into not-so-big projects, small projects and eventually completed projects. Help your child make a list of things to do to get started: review the assignment to make sure you understand it, call a friend, put together a team, do some research, ask for help, plan it out...the list can be short and to the point, so the child is not spending a lot of time making a list. Call it a plan of attack. Check off items when complete. Get to work! Simply starting a project, chipping away at it one step at a time, immediately makes it feel less daunting.

5. *List the Pro's and Con's.* Sometimes indecision turns to inaction and that can seem negative. If your teen stumbles making a big decision, a good skill to teach them is to make a list of the pros and cons of the outcome. Maybe the decision is, let's say for argument's sake, to join a sports team. If they join, make a list of all the Pro's (get in shape, make new friends, have fun…) and a list of all the Con's (may have to give up another activity, lost family time, less time for friends, less time to study….) Sometimes the decision is made clear simply by doing the exercise. A word of advice, parents: your child may need help in completing this dual-sided list—it's a skill that has to be learned and practiced. Get both parents involved if possible; maybe include an older sibling if they've been through something similar.

6. *Envision the positive outcome.* Okay, here's a more grown-up response to a negative outlook. It's simple to explain, yet difficult to execute. Envision the positive outcome. Think positively and see the expected result happening. Actually talk about it, verbally, out loud. If a major test looms, have the teen see themselves studying, understanding, asking questions, writing down correct answers, and doing well on the test. Repeat the exercise at least three times each time you "envision the outcome." Do this several times a day until the test. Seeing yourself succeed in the future can change the future. What you envision will come to pass. It actually programs the mind to settle for nothing less than the outcome you want and see. So, envision the positive!

7. *Trust in the future.* Many times, a murky future breeds a negative outlook. Nobody can predict everything that will happen tomorrow or the next day and everyone has bad things happen. Bad things *do* happen to good people. That's part of life. God doesn't promise that life will always be easy, just that he will always be with us. Teach your child that trusting in the

future—trusting that more good things will happen than bad—combats the murkiness of not knowing. Use phrases like "everything will be okay" and "life has a way of working itself out" and "we're in this together" and "I've got your back on this one" and "don't worry, you can handle it." Make up your own pet phrases for your children. Repeat often. Reassurance leads to confidence.

8. *Here is another suggestion:* The brain is like a powerful supercomputer. It can work while you do something else. If you have a problem with which you are struggling, write the problem down on a piece of paper before going to bed and let it go. Once you have a good night's rest you will be surprised how many times you will wake up and have a fresh, positive outlook in the morning. Your brain has been working on that problem while you've been snoozing. Often that's enough to distill the solution—and out it pops.

Parenting Tip

Play "What If" with your kids. If your child slips into negative talk, switch it around with a game of "What If". A few examples might help.

If your child is a "negative nelly" about a subject at school in which they are not experiencing much success, ask: what if we found you a tutor? What if we helped you every night for two weeks? What if you asked your teacher for help? What if you formed a study group, to meet at our house, and consisting of a few kids who are stars in that subject? The "what ifs" are endless. The goal is to turn the frown upside down. Turn the negative to positive.

If your son or daughter feels dejection about a person of the opposite sex in which they are interested. "What If" questions to ask: What if you asked them over to our house to study or have a meal? What if you said to them that you liked a certain outfit or hairstyle? What if you told them you admired something they said to another to pump them up or encourage the other person? What if you asked them out? (Oh, my!) What if, what if, what if.

Fill in the positive possibilities when your teen sees only the negative or nothing at all.

Parents Prayer

I know that you are a good God, only wanting the best for me. I know that negative thought does not come from you, Lord. I know you never deceive or confuse me. I believe you when you say that I can ask you for anything. Help me to see the positive in any situation, to see you in every detail. Keep my eyes focused on your heavenly glory. Thank you, sweet Jesus. Amen.

Stretch the Strategy

1. How did your upbringing shape your outlook in life? Who around you as you grew into adulthood impacted you the most? And how did they do it?
2. What strategies do you employ now to solve dilemmas?
3. How much do you trust God to take care of you in the future?

#29

Teach Your Teens to Explore and Identify Their Feelings

I suppose I've always done my share of crying, especially when there's no other way to contain my feelings. I know that men ain't supposed to cry, but I think that's wrong. Crying's always been a way for me to get things out which are buried deep, deep down. When I sing, I often cry. Crying is feeling, and feeling is being human. Oh yes, I cry.

—Ray Charles

We're going to get a little "touchy-feely" in this chapter.

The teen years explode with new experiences and challenges, shifting viewpoints and feedback, and changing minds and bodies. Hormones kick in. School gets harder; subjects become more demanding. Friendships that worked in middle school now seem tricky or taxing. New feelings creep in. Remember, this is all part of normal adolescent development.

By helping teens identify their feelings we help them

understand what they are experiencing. We explore our feelings to know our actions and reactions to circumstances. We look inside to see how we are reacting to a situation—to better understand our life, our bodies, our outlooks, and our responses.

Our feelings affect our bodies—our nervous system, heart rate, perspiration, and even shaking or trembling. They exist in our bodies and make our bodies react in new and strange ways. Feelings affect our perception of what's happening around us. If we feel nervous, normal situations can become scary. Feelings can be contagious and can influence others around you. (Parents, you know this, don't you?) Your fear can be transferred to your friends or siblings. Now everyone in the situation is fearful. Uh, oh.

You can experience several feelings at the same time, like anger and fear, but also like anger and love. That's confusing, isn't it? How in the world does that happen? And which feeling is stronger? Which one will prevail? Which one will win?

Feelings are not right or wrong, good or bad. They just exist. The whole gamut—the whole shebang of feelings—you will experience. Every one. And suppressing our feelings, the more common way to handle them, fuels consequences. Suppressed feelings can turn into uneasiness, being ill at ease, which is just another way of saying disease. Worry turns into ulcers or headaches. Anger turns into upset stomachs or worse. But let's not spend too much time talking about all the bad things that holding your feelings in could produce. Let's work through them.

First, help your teen to express feelings. Ask them the question: "How does that make you feel?" Answers that are nebulous—like "good" or "bad" or "nice" or "okay"—don't work because they're not definitive enough. In fact, you could make a list of feelings for your child so she or he knows what they might be. Here's a partial list; feel free to add to it as the teen expresses one.

- Fearful
- Anxious
- Scared
- Nervous
- Excited
- Guilty
- Confident
- Sympathetic
- Thrilled
- Peaceful
- Certain
- Impulsive
- Curious
- Intense
- Loved
- Satisfied
- Thankful
- Lucky
- Encouraged
- Blessed
- Unique
- Rebellious
- Bright
- Surprised
- Fascinated
- Snoopy
- Tender
- Comforted
- Daring
- Brave

You can search online for a "list of feelings" and build your own. Once your child expresses a feeling, you can ask them to find a place in their body that is affected by the feeling. Fear can show up in tight muscles. Love can be felt in the heart. Nervousness in the stomach or bowels. This exercise will help a teen realize that the body holds feelings. And once the feeling is expressed, they may experience how a body can release a feeling, too.

Then talk it out. Remind them that feelings are normal but may not determine outcomes. We are all entitled to our feelings, and you should never tell a child (or an adult for that matter, goodness sakes) they should not feel the way they feel.

Just point out that because, for instance, you feel scared, it doesn't necessarily mean something is scary. Because you feel guilty doesn't mean there is something to feel guilty about.

Teens can write about their feelings, too. By keeping a journal or a diary, teens can express feelings they don't have to share with anyone, including parents if they wish. It's a good way to get feelings out and down on paper (preferably not on a computer because those are not secure.) Reviewing them from time to time will teach a teen what to expect in the future, as far as feelings go, and secondly, to not let feelings run their lives. They can look back at a feeling, like fear, and realize that the fear wasn't warranted, that things just worked out for the best, no matter whether they had that particular feeling of fear or not.

This book won't work through the tough feelings like anger, guilt, or sadness. Obviously, if your child continually feels a particular way—not every once in a while, but constantly—then get some professional help dealing with those feelings. You should never discount a feeling. They are real and if they persist, pervade, and penetrate your child to the point of distress or discomfort, take action. Find help. If you are not great at expressing feelings (I'm speaking to dads mostly, but moms are not exempt), get some professional help if you need it. No harm there; no feelings of inadequacy in the parent, please.

In my own life, I've had to develop the ability to confront and identify my feelings. For too long, I suppressed and ignored them. Guilt and shame were my two big anchors. They weighed on me heavily and negatively affected my family and my health. And it certainly wasn't easy to explore those feelings; it took hard work. I'm not going into all the details here, but you can read my book *Lumberjack Jesus* to learn how I handled it. (Hint, Jesus led the way and became my coach, teacher, and confidant.) Maybe it's enough to say here that if you help your child explore their feelings at a young age, they won't suffer as much as I did by their suppression.

One of the best ways to live a resilient and confident life is to be able to explore, identify, and let go of feelings. And of course, in some cases, to recapture them—the good feelings—the love, happy, satisfied, thankful feelings. Just don't let your child be ruled by feelings. Remind them often that feelings are not facts, they're just feelings. They don't have to "control" feelings—just the exercise of learning to identify them is usually enough to handle at their tender, developing age.

Parenting Tip

To help kids identify feelings, let's make a game of it. We could call it "Feelings Faces" or maybe you come up with a name on your own. Here's how it works. As the parent, you ask the child to name a feeling. Then you make a face to capture that feeling. Don't be afraid to overdo it, exaggerate the face, like a funny face. Because games are supposed to be fun, right? Then get the child involved. You could even incorporate body movements that depict the feeling. For instance, sad could not just be a frown but could include slumped shoulders, a deep sigh, shuffling steps. And don't concentrate on a feeling that the teen has exhibited lately. Do more happy feeling faces than sad! And most of all, have fun playing!

Parents Prayer

I want to feel your love, Jesus. I desire to express my love back to you. I want you to open my heart to the things that break yours and help me to feel your love and compassion for my fellow man. Teach me to express what I'm feeling so I can better communicate to you and my family. Thank you, sweet Jesus. Amen.

Stretch the Strategy

1.   What feelings do you regularly express? (You might make a list and then compare your list to a similar one your spouse makes for you. The differences could be enlightening.)
2.   Did your parents encourage you to express your feelings?
3.   Do you have feelings that you are unwilling to share with God?

#30
Coach Your Teens to Communicate Without Using Digital

People will come to adore the technologies that undo their capacities to think.

—Neil Postman, *Amusing Ourselves to Death*

This American teen generation communicates better with their mobile phones than with their mouths. On the surface, this may not seem like a big deal. But studies show that once these children enter the workplace, it's a *very* big deal.

Millennials have been accused of craving instant gratification. But even teens born after the Millennial generation (1982-2003) have been seduced to expect it. Digital delivers that. A few examples:

- If they want a reaction from a friend, about anything, they send a text. Boom! Text back.
- If they want to see a movie, they don't need to look up start times at theaters or plan their day around going to the movies, they stream it on their tablet.

This instant gratification in and of itself isn't bad. But it teaches that anything is available instantly. When that generation and your American teenager find out that is not true, they are ill-prepared to cope.

Two specific situations—one first experienced in the teen years, and one realized later as young adults enter the workforce—illustrate the point.

Relationships. As teens begin to develop relationships with other teens and experiment with dating, they have been trained to expect communication to flow easily and effortlessly—because it does on a cellphone. (LOL, shm, imho, cute, ... whatever.) They are clueless about how to deal with the messiness of relationships—the ups and downs, the lack of talking and expressing feelings, the fear of saying the wrong thing or having it misinterpreted. That's why many junior and senior high relationships dissolve so quickly. They simply have not learned to talk with their mouths. They have been using their thumbs too long. And when they put the phone down and look into somebody's eyes, they are lost. They cannot communicate.

You may say that teens have always had troubling communicating in boy/girl relationships. Yes, you're right—and it's even worse now.

Work Satisfaction. When young adults programmed to expect instant gratification enter the workforce, they expect instant success. They want to "make a difference" or "have an impact" at the company they work for—and they want to do it right now. When this doesn't happen—and it rarely does—they become disillusioned and disappointed. After all, they have led a life that says they can receive immediate satisfaction. In the realm of career, you have to work at success; you have to acquire skills to meet expectations; you have to learn from your mistakes. All of that takes time.

With most corporations now often more concerned with making their quarterly numbers and less concerned with nurturing and training young adults, this realization can be shocking. Young adults new to the work environment don't know how to communicate with their boss or their cohorts. It probably contributes to some degree why more young adults in their twenties are back home living with their parents, some without jobs or careers.

Here are a few ideas—call them rules if you want to—to help your teen learn to live in a world not focused on the phone.

- The phone does not accompany the teen to: the dinner table, a restaurant, or a movie theater. This will be very hard to enforce. Start early, when the teen first gets a phone. Enforce often. But I wouldn't restrict the use of a cell phone on a date. I am concerned about safety on this one. What if the teen gets in a situation and needs you? The cell phone is a way to reach out for help in this case.

- When a group of friends gather together, phones don't go. (Or maybe just one, for emergencies.) How would the teen with the group feel if one of them is on the phone, texting another friend who isn't there in person? Left out, ignored. If teens are in your home, have them leave their phones either at home or collect them when they arrive. Have them communicate face to face. You may have to make a game of this because, face it, teens are literally addicted to these devices.

- If you need to punish your teen for anything, make the punishment a loss of phone privileges. This will teach that having a phone is a privilege and that they can live without it—at least for short periods of time.

- Delay giving a phone to a teen until a more appropriate age. They will begin asking for one early in life "because all their friends have one," which is not true—you know that, right, parents? Their friends don't all have a phone, and that is not a good reason to give them one anyway. You and your spouse decide the appropriate age, then add a year or two.

- Allow the teen to take the phone to school but only for security purposes. Yes, you are the parent, and you make the rules. If you want to get in touch with them or they with you, they can send a text or receive one, even a phone call in emergencies. (We have to let our kids have phones in schools now, just because of the recent history of school violence. Darn.) But find a way to restrict their communication with friends while at school. I know, they'll complain and do their best to find ways to deceive you but teach them to use their voice and their ears for listening at school as much as possible. In fact, in some schools, once classes begin the phones are not permitted to be out unless the teacher is permitting use of a smart phone app as part of instruction.

- Monitor their phone. Find a way. This is not an invasion of privacy. It is your right and duty as a parent. And make it clear that this is *your* phone on loan to the teen. If the teen balks at this, you will have to reinforce the rules of authority in the household. Then you may have to take the phone away for a period of time. Obviously, this could produce friction between parent and teen. So be it. Get to work and be a parent. I know, it's not always as easy job. Sorry.

- No using the phone while doing homework. The phone can be turned off and stored someplace other than the homework spot.

- No charging the phone in the teenager's bedroom overnight. Find a place in the home for all phones to be charged, like the kitchen, and put the little buggers (the phones, that is) to bed there. Once again, this will be challenged by your teen. They will despise this rule, especially if you haven't enforced something like this in the past. Be ready, parents, for some blowback here.

- No phone communication after a certain time at night. Maybe nine p.m. works; a little later as the teen gets older.

Please remember, texting is not full communication. The "voice" of a text can be very shallow, unable to relay all the nuances of actual talking, like inflection, tone, authority, and eye rolls. My daughter, now in her early thirties, still uses the words "talk" and "text" interchangeably. She will often say she talked to someone when she means she texted with that person. You may have to remind your teen they are two distinct words—and point out the real benefits of actually talking with your voice.

The graphic designer who helped design my website saw an early version of this chapter in a blog post I wrote. She has twin teenage girls. Here's her response to the post about this topic of digital addiction:

"My girls text me to ask when dinner will be ready instead of coming out of their rooms. They are afraid to call someone on the phone because they don't know what to say. When their friends come over, all the kids sit

around texting together. When I give one of their friends a ride home, they sit in the backseat texting and never say a word to me or to the person sitting next to them. It is a problem!"

We must teach our children to communicate with their mouths and their brains. We have to tell them the perils of constant digital use. Parents, you may have grown up in front of a television and that probably produced bad habits and curbed your ability to connect with people. Today's teens are even more addicted to their devices than you were to that box. They first begin to suffer with this as a child. It will affect all of their relationships and certainly could impact their careers and their ability to achieve and succeed. Okay, scared yet? Good. Now go talk with your teen—and leave your phone behind.

Parenting Tip

If you don't believe the evils of social media, pick up a copy of the book *The Happiness Effect: How Social Media is Driving a Generation to Appear Perfect at Any Cost* by Donna Freitas. The findings by the author, who interviewed hundreds of college-age kids, might be surprising, even shocking. It's not primarily the sexting or cyber bullying we should be concerned about, but rather, the drive to look perfectly happy at all times. Her conclusions indicate that many young adults are more concerned about appearing happy than actually *being* happy and how that mentality encourages nonstop peer-to-peer comparison and pressure. It's a fascinating, yet scary. read. (And yes, we should be concerned about sexting and cyber bullying, too.)

Bonus Tip: I love this book—you may, too: *52 Ways to Connect with Your Smartphone Obsessed Kid* by Jonathan McKee.

It's chock-full of ways to engage with your children and distract them from their digital world.

Extra Bonus Tip: Be radical. As a family, declare a "no screens" day. No phones, TV, or computers—no interaction with anything that has a screen. This will take ingenuity, planning, and guts. Maybe do this one day a month. You'll survive and so will your teen. But you may initially have withdrawals, like an addiction. I know families that do this one day a week, one weekend a month, and one week a year. Radical, huh? But you may be surprised at how peaceful life becomes without the constant assault of digital devices.

Parents Prayer

This seems bigger than I can handle at times, Lord. Help me find a way to overcome the world. Show me how to lean on you for guidance and direction. I want to rely on you for help in communicating with my children how much I love them, how real my love is, and how dedicated I am to them. Give me ideas to banish technology, if only for a while, as I talk and pray with my children. Thank you, sweet Jesus. Amen.

Stretch the Strategy

1. What are the rules in your family concerning the use of phones, TVs, and computers?
2. Does anything need to be altered about those rules?
3. How addicted are you to your portable devices?
4. What is your view of social media and its effect on teens?

#31

Teach Your Teens to Live in the Present

Be true to yourself, help others, make each day your masterpiece, make friendship a fine art, drink deeply from good books— especially the Bible—build a shelter against a rainy day, give thanks for your blessings and pray for guidance every day.

—John Wooden

hat?! You say? *I cannot even get my teen to live anywhere else other than the present!* I know, I know, it's a fine line. We want our children to live for today and not worry about the future, and yet we want them to plan for their futures. What to do?

We discussed earlier about not sweating the small stuff— not worrying about things they shouldn't or can't control. It's a skill most of us need to work on. Some teens naturally tend *not* to worry—at all. Good for them. Encourage them to continue along that trajectory.

But there is a flip side to not worrying. It's "living for today." To be able to live in the moment means that you enjoy life, whatever life offers up. You don't shy away from what's right in front of you—opportunities, chances, hurdles, challenges, fears. You barge ahead; you plug along if you have to, but you keep moving forward. You do not back away or back down or give up.

That can be effortless for some teenagers because of their need for exploration, when what's right in front of them is:

- Exciting
- New
- A little daring
- Hopeful

But it is much more difficult to stay the course and live in the present if what they face is:

- Challenging
- Fearful
- Hard
- Unexplainable

Sometimes teens will let their rebel side show by *not* doing things that are:

- Good for them
- Suggested by parents
- Traditional (seen as old school or antiquated)

All of the above reactions are very natural and acceptable for teenagers. Parents, sometimes if you tell them what they should do, they don't—or they feel like they want to do the exact opposite. Don't drink alcohol, so they want to drink. Don't smoke, so they want to try cigarettes. Don't do drugs, so what could it hurt, let's try drugs.

My message here is *don't preach, teach.*

Here are a few ideas to encourage teens and young adults to live in the moment.

1. ***Allow them to say YES.*** This reiterates the earlier instruction to say YES more than NO. Don't always have your fallback position be NO. Allow them to say YES to opportunities. If you need to think about a decision or talk to your spouse or discuss with your teen, by all means, go for it. But you can also make a quick, informed decision and evaluate later how it worked out. You'll be surprised at how often the teen benefits from the experience of trying something new.

2. ***Encourage them to say YES.*** You do not have to encourage them to be so daring they become irresponsible, but if you encourage them to take chances and calculated risks, they may find that there is no harm in jumping in, the water's just fine. Be sure to offer risk evaluation and counseling—that's always helpful even if it's not always appreciated. Just don't go too far—a little steering is good; micro-management isn't so helpful. We want to teach them to make informed decisions and rest easy with the consequences.

3. ***Present opportunities.*** Don't assume your teen will always find opportunities in life. They can get bogged down in schoolwork, friends, and video games. Do you remember when you first suggested they try _____? (You fill in the blank, for instance, soccer, piano, singing, lemonade stands, summer camp, avocado, fried bologna on white bread.) They may have resisted, relented and—then when they tried it, enjoyed themselves. So, offer up suggestions.

4. ***Never let them give in to the thinking "it's too tough."*** There will be opportunities that scare them. The next challenge in math or science; playing "up" in sports to the next level;

learning a musical instrument; asking that redhead for a date. Encourage them to bust through the fear and go for it anyway. Use the old reliable, "What's the worst that could happen?" line and show them how to concentrate on the "best that could happen" possibility. A little bit of failure is okay, and it's often better than the feelings you get when you don't even try. Regret can be a terrible feeling to live with.

5. ***Do not let them get away with the excuse "I'm too tired."*** Sure, teens can be overcommitted, and they need their sleep. On the other hand, they are extremely resilient and can be relentless when on target, doing something they really want or love. "I'm too tired" becomes an old excuse—a fallback position when they don't want to try—and should be acknowledged only when you see signs of exhaustion. Don't let them use it simply as a reason not to experience something new and different.

6. ***Don't always emphasize work, work, work.*** Encourage play, too. Play lets teens be free and experiment. That's why they love games, even games they make up. Video games, backyard games, it doesn't matter. Encourage play and watch your teen thrive. (I know, some of you are saying, *all my teen does is play*! Again, please find the balance that works for your individual ball of energy.) A recent Harvard Medical School report studied the play habits of kids. The results were shocking. Between 1981 and 1997, the time children actually played declined by 25 percent. Increased school demands, the relentless lure of social media, and parents who loaded kids up with organized activities contributed to the fall off. Increased academic pressures have left 30 percent of kindergartens in the U.S. without recess. Kindergartens! If you are parents who load kids with structured activities looking to give your child a leg up in a competitive world, do more research into the benefits of play. It builds resilience and confidence—at times better than

studying and working.

7. *Have fun while driving*. When learning to drive, teens want to do one thing: drive the car. Make it a game and make it fun. One day, turn right at all stop signs and turn left at all stop lights. Just see where you end up. Then one day take surface streets instead of the freeway or interstate. Don't always use GPS to figure out exactly where you are. Let the teen figure it out; help them if needed. It will give a sense that it's quite all right to not know where you are every second of every day. The following day tell the teen to stop somewhere they've always wanted to stop or someplace you've been "meaning" to stop for some time. Then see what develops. Could be the zoo, the park, the candy store, the theater, wherever. And finally, instruct the teen to just go "nowhere." Stop when you get there. Talk about the day. Enjoy each other's company. Have fun. (If you don't have a car, this works with walking or taking the bus, too.)

Living in the present, in the moment, allows teens to enjoy life and not fear it. It trains them to expect the unexpected and to not get frustrated by what happens unpredictably. It helps to redefine challenges and hurdles as possibilities and opportunities. It makes the teen tap into their creativity and talents to solve situations and to thrive. Accepting the present trains them to be resilient, to not give in, to stay on task, and to succeed. America will need those types of adults in the future, won't we? For sure.

Parenting Tip

Here's an interesting twist on parenting. Ask your teens how you can be a better parent. Be prepared for some off the wall input. Be open to hearing how you could be better in the moment—as encourager, coach, judge, policeman—in the many roles you play. The technique may open up new ways to communicate with your teen. And remember, you don't have to be perfect as a parent, just as your child does not have to be perfect as a kid. You can learn, too. Don't be afraid of encouraging these talks. You may well have to defend your actions—but that's fine—because now your teen will not only understand your reasoning and logic, but they'll begin to understand how hard it can be at times to be a parent. I like this idea because it empowers your child to provide some feedback to you as a parent.

Parents Prayer

Good Lord, help me to learn to be the best parent I can. Let me leave parental mistakes behind and learn from them. Encourage me to forgive myself and forge ahead, not looking back but moving forward. I want to continue improving and living each day to the best of my ability—and for your glory. Thank you, sweet Jesus. Amen.

Stretch the Strategy

1. How much do you enjoy "play" in your life?
2. Do you fully understand the benefits of play?
3. In what area in your life could you play a little more?

#32

Show Your Teens the Benefits of a Lifetime of Learning

Education is what remains after one has forgotten what one has learned in school.

—Albert Einstein

Twenty percent of teenagers do not finish high school in America. You may be shocked at that figure, but in comparison, it's not too horrible. The statistics are much lower in other parts of the world. In countries like Haiti, for instance, less than two percent complete high school. Of course, not all learning happens in schools.

Sometimes, young adults leave learning behind when they finish formal schooling. They may need to learn certain job skills when they become employed, but real learning gets neglected, like a smelly sweatshirt thrown to the back of the closet. This can produce adults who rely on television or the internet for not only entertainment but for education, if you can call it that. Search engines pry open knowledge, a wonderful tool to learn some basics. Shocker: not everything found online is true. Did you know that just about anyone can author a Wikipedia page? I've done it myself. (I wrote exactly what I wanted, with no critique or oversight, and they published immediately. Scary, huh? That happened a few years ago; maybe it's changed by now.) The digital world does not dispense all wisdom.

This need to be a lifelong learner may be a difficult lesson to impart on the teenagers under your influence. They may not want to hear it—because it's hammered into them daily in school. But, as parents, we want to not only prepare our children to be responsible and self-reliant young adults, but to engage learning so they can foster those traits throughout their lives. Think back to what you knew when you were in your late teenage years, eighteen or nineteen. Not what you *thought* you knew—but what you actually knew. You still had a lot to learn about being a high-functioning adult, didn't you? Me, too.

Consider these ideas to nurture that love of learning your teenagers will need throughout life.

1. ***Read to them at a young age.*** You can even start as early as pre-birth, reading while they're still in the womb. Read, read, read to them. Make it fun, make it exciting. Really get into it. See smiles on your child's face when they listen. You can tell them stories, too, but if they get to handle the book, turn the page, and see the pictures, the love of reading is engrained in them from the get-go. And reading is *the* essential tool of learning.

2. ***Continue reading to them in their teen years.*** Maybe not just entire books. Articles, quotes, news items, tidbits— something they can listen to quickly. Obviously, you will have to find things to read that excite a teenager. Easy-peasy. If they like science find a science article about a cool planet or electricity or thunderstorms or bugs or, well, science provides an endless pool of topics. They like history? Find a short book on the Civil War and read about the battle of Gettysburg or

ancient Rome or Woodstock or the Space Race. Do they like video games? Find resources that explain how computer code is written or computer chips are produced. How about sports? Find articles that discuss training techniques or nutritional tactics of elite athletes. Do they like movies and TV? No, don't read *People* magazine! Read to them about science or history or anything but movies and TV, please!

3. **Teach them to question the facts.** Contrary to your belief, kids do not need to believe everything their parents tell them. What they really need is a brain that can figure out right from wrong, good from bad, and true from false. You may not want to raise kids that always question Mom and Dad, but it's not a bad thing to have conversations that stretch your children's thinking and yours. Find controversial topics where an argument can be made from either side of the issue. This will not be difficult in today's America. Talk about them. Discuss both sides and if you need to, become the devil's advocate to show why both sides matter. They may learn to search more deeply for facts and answers. Or they may learn that life is not always black and white, but rather, muted shades of gray. All good things to learn. Along with this, be sure to teach them that they must evaluate the source of information as they form an opinion.

4. **Show them what you're learning at your age.** Did you just take a webinar to better understand Facebook advertising? Share a bit about that with your teens. Did you find a Tony Robbins book (or video or audio) about creating your own destiny or a Max Lucado piece about faith or a Brene Brown TED talk about vulnerability? Short conversations with your teen can ignite more learning or plant the seed for future investigation. And let's be truthful, if they don't see you putting this trait of lifelong learning into practice, they will be a whole lot less likely to jump on the bookmobile. You don't just sit in

front of the TV every evening, all evening, do you?

5. **Show them how to read for pleasure.** Okay, this may take some ingenuity. Teens and young adults often don't embark on pleasure reading until the crush of "study reading" relinquishes. For some that means after college. So, reading for pleasure may only happen in short spurts. Inexpensive magazines provide a great source of pleasure, if you find the one your teen will read. Search for them. And no, no *Us* or *Tiger Beat!* Finding books that teens like and have the time to read presents challenges. News flash: Libraries house a wonderful source of books and most towns have at least one. Visit and grab a bunch of books. If one doesn't measure up, you don't have to finish reading it. I won't tell and nobody will know. Vacations provide plenty of time to read for pleasure, so have your teen take a book along—printed, digital, or audio.

6. *Introduce them to the audiobook.* So, your teens are not good readers? No problem, the audiobook delivers. Download, plug in, and enjoy. Just make sure they aren't listening to Taylor Swift or Kanye West when they claim to be getting into Charles Dickens or Clive Cussler.

7. *Watch TV.* Did I really just write that? Yes, I did, but with a caveat. Please don't spend your time watching reruns of *Seinfeld* or *The Big Bang Theory* (that's not about science; it's all about horny young adults). Try PBS or NatGeo or other educational channels. Just pick something they'll like. If they aren't into botany, maybe the *Secret Life of Plants* will not keep them from dozing.

8. *Get engaged in their schoolwork.* Maybe you can't help them with calculus but in subjects that you can, discuss what they're studying. Find out what they're learning—you might be surprised, either at how much they know or how little actual thinking is going on. Either way, if you engage in the process, you can help steer them and guide them. (You also may be very

surprised at what their textbooks are teaching your teenagers. And it may give you the opportunity to present the flip side of what textbook publishers view as timely and relevant curriculum.)

9. ***Introduce them to podcasts*** that interest you. They are probably using them in school.

Learning doesn't stop when the school bell rings. It stops when there is nothing left to learn. As in never. Even well-established practices like medicine, for example, change constantly. If you thought you knew everything about medicine ten years ago, you'd be woefully behind today. Scientific discoveries happen every day. What we thought we knew about many different subjects and ideas no longer hold water. Technology enables the world to move at record speed. You have more computing power in your phone these days than you did in your personal computer a few years ago. Learning should keep up, keep pace. It can also be used for knocking down walls of misinformation, building a better future, discovering new cures, and unleashing the power of the human brain. Keep studying, keep learning!

Parenting Tip

Get into the habit of giving books as presents. I know, books can seem outdated, archaic, or passé to some teens. But eventually, when they don't have to spend their valuable time reading textbooks, they might just get into books. The key to this one is: they have to be fun or interesting. Those are the two rules. Fun or interesting. Of course, that depends on the reader, doesn't it? For instance, many comedians write books. I always found Dave Barry to write very funny books. How about Amy Schumer or Ellen DeGeneres? Interesting can take on another aspect, depending on what fascinates your child. But, please, stay away from long, boring texts. You can try fiction, too, as the Young Adult genre produces many interesting titles. (Warning: some are about werewolves, sorcerers, vampires, and other otherworldly beings, so be wary and scrutinize.) Keep experimenting. And remember, you don't have to purchase all these books to begin. Just visit your local library. When you find a genre your teen really likes, then the gift of a book is right on target. Remember to sign the book, as a gift from you, and date it. I still have several in my personal library given to me by my grandparents many moons ago.

Parents Prayer

I want to continue to learn and grow, Lord. Show me where and what to study, who to emulate, and how to keep learning more. Open my mind and heart to new possibilities and ideas—even miracles! I know that you are the best teacher, the master teacher, the one who can teach me what I need to know. Thank you, sweet Jesus. Amen.

Stretch the Strategy

1. What's one topic that you'd like to learn more about this year?
2. How many books did you read last year?
3. How much TV do you watch a day?

#33
Help Your Teens Develop a Vision for Their Successful Future

My advice to any young person at the beginning of their career is to try to look for the mere outlines of big things with their fresh, untrained, and unprejudiced mind.

—Hans Selye

To counterbalance and bolster the skill to "live life in the present," teens need to be taught the skill of envisioning a bright and successful future. This may be a God-given ability in some young adults, but for most, you'll need to take the lead on this learning, parents.

The two key words in this chapter title are "vision" and "successful." A vision is not a dream, although the two can be interpreted as similar. A dream is whimsical, comes upon you unexpectedly, and can float away as quickly as clouds on a windy day. The vision I'm referring to here is not simply an awake dream.

Call it eyesight for the future.

A *vision* takes time to develop, incorporates your talents and gifts, focuses on your likes and abilities, and has a path to completion. The end outcome of a vision may change as young adults grow and mature—in tweaks, adjustments, refinements, and even overhauls—but change and growth only adds to the power of the vision. It's never too early in a young adult life to talk about developing a vision for the future.

If your child balks at the word vision, use "plan," knowing that plans change but having a plan keeps you on course. I've seen the phrase "life plan" bantered about but that might seem pretty huge—*like for the rest of my life?*—in a teenager's mind. Don't saddle your child with something so big and daunting that they resist just on the perception that it's too overwhelming to even think about.

I can hear them say: *I'm just a kid!*

Children, teenagers, and young adults may not possess the ability to envision the future. We've discussed this before. That ability is often a learned behavior. Envisioning success in the future may not come naturally. (This is not a book about developing a positive outlook on life and the influence of positive thinking, but you can find those books if you look.) You could start off having the teen practice visioning in these following situations before they move on to producing a successful plan for their future.

- Practice seeing themselves doing well on an upcoming test or assignment.
- Practice seeing success on the sports field for an upcoming contest.
- Practice seeing themselves asking that boy or girl for a date without nervousness—and the date saying yes!
- Practice seeing the day turning out fine.

The word *successful* hones in on possibilities. After all, isn't the future for teenagers to make as they see it? Aren't the possibilities almost endless? Yes, I know, the economics of today's youth in certain sectors of American society limits their options. But that should not limit their possibilities. If your teen cannot envision a life of success (happiness, fulfillment, purpose, achievement, independence) then we have to steer them to those possibilities.

Maybe a few tips will help:

- *Broaden their possibilities.* If they only want to work at a fast-food restaurant, they need help in developing a vision of where else they could work. Take them out and show them possibilities, new work environs, other jobs they don't know about. Make a list of possible jobs and post it in their room; add to the list regularly. You can begin with both starter jobs and career paths. If they want to work in fast food, help them set a goal to work in management for a fast-food store. This might lead to a career owning their own restaurant.

- *Shift their thinking.* If they only think of "less successful" then shift that to "more successful." Raise the bar. Find successful people who have overcome big odds to make their vision a reality. Find books that feature these people. See the movie *The Pursuit of Happyness* with Will Smith. Study people like the comedian Steve Harvey as role models—you will find his story fascinating and relatable. Find and use inspiration where you can, but never allow a vision to take seed in your child that limits their potential or downgrades their talents.

Next, let's discuss one way to put a successful vision or plan together. Many different ways exist, so if this one doesn't work, find one that does. Be relentless to find a process that clicks with your teen.

1. Get your child to talk about their future.
2. Review their gifts, talents, and abilities.
3. Find vocations, at least ten, that match their likes and abilities.
4. Talk to friends or relatives who work in those matching vocations.
5. Uncover the education and training needed for several vocations that interest your child.
6. Continually remind your teen that they will have to study and work hard to achieve their plan.
7. Begin to write the vision down on paper in one page or less. Or a collage-filled vision board for the more creative or visual teen.
8. The vision plan may include these sections: Vision, Talents I Possess, Vocations that Interest Me, Vocations I Would Love to Do, People to Talk To, Help I Need, Things to Research…
9. Periodically, for instance once a quarter, review, tweak, and add to the plan.
10. Make sure the vision is for a *successful* future.
11. Do not settle for futures that are decent, good, adequate, achievable, make sense, or any such mediocre descriptions.
12. Help your child where needed.
13. Never interject negativity or skepticism; a dose of reality is fine.
14. Never let your child give up. Never. Never.

Notice I didn't include a section about money or salary. If you simply allow a teen to focus on this aspect of a vocation, their plan could dissolve quickly. They don't have much experience knowing what's a good salary or a bad one. They drastically underestimate what money is needed to live a life they want. They can automatically overestimate their worth or value. And they lose focus on what excites them, what they are passionate about in life, and lean towards "making money." Remember and remind your teen:

- *Do what you love to do, and the money will follow.*

- *Be in love with what you are doing, and money takes a back seat.*

- *Be true to yourself, and money will help you achieve your future, not dictate it.*

- *You can always work a "job" for money, but never plan a future vocation by what it pays.*

As loving and attentive as my parents were, they never helped me think much about the future. They sent me to college and that was a great experience, but it didn't prepare me well for a successful career. It wasn't until I was in my late twenties that I found mentors who helped me plan and work toward a life that thrilled me. Consequently, most of the help I offered my kids, I'm chagrined to admit, came when they were looking for their first jobs. That's a little late.

Successful futures happen for many people by chance. Some get lucky. Others work hard and it falls into place. Many are prepared when opportunity knocks. Others are introduced to the right people at the right time. All of these possibilities exist and cannot be discounted. But truly enlightened individuals use their God-given gifts and talents, their likes and wants, and their practiced abilities and strengths to envision, plan, and find a future that delivers everything they want and need for a successful life. Sounds delightful, doesn't it?

Parenting Tip

Think "Career Day" at home. I speak to mostly junior high students as a volunteer during "career day" at local schools. I put together a PowerPoint presentation on a thumb drive because most classes now have a laptop available for projection in the class. I talk about what I did during certain stages of my careers in sales, marketing, advertising, and writing. I concentrate on what a typical day is like, the skills I need to succeed, and how my passion for my work overrides any illusion of moneymaking. I use those techniques to introduce teens to possibilities.

You could first begin to have these conversations with your children about your own jobs. But then expand. Invite friends and neighbors to dinner and prep them that your kids would love to hear about what they do for a living. You might give the guests some pointers of how to prepare (formal training they received, why they wanted this job, skills needed, typical day, frustrations, competition for those jobs, and benefits.) No presentation is needed, just conversation. Make sure your kids are on board with this. They cannot seem disinterested, bored, or lackadaisical. If they have to invent enthusiasm for a job that doesn't sound so interesting, that's a great skill to practice, too.

This inter-generational mingling—teenagers with older adults—ignites benefits for both generations. The youngsters learn valuable lessons, and the oldsters re-engage with segments of society from whom they may have become detached. Much research has revealed how this generational mingling produces value, as evidenced by inviting retirees into preschools, for instance, to read to the children. Both kids and seniors love it.

Parents Prayer

Jesus, help me to help my children see a successful, fulfilling future. Keep me away from the trap of procrastination, depression, and unwillingness to try. Let me embrace new ideas and pass along the joy of looking for a fresh approach. Help me paint a picture of heaven so I see the possibilities of eternity. Thank you, sweet Jesus. Amen.

Stretch the Strategy

1. What is your plan for your future? How well does your spouse know what your plan is?
2. How often do you tweak that plan?
3. How much do you trust God to guide you, bless you, provide for you, and be with you as you plan your future?

Conclusion

Wow, 33 strategies to teach self-reliance, confidence, and responsibility! We've reached the end. I could have come up with a few more, but by now, I think you have the picture. And I know you're busy being a parent.

Here's a suggestion: do them all. All 33. Don't skimp, don't cut corners. They are all critical because I pared down the list to the most vital ones.

If you cannot manage all 33, do your best. That's all I can ask. But just think, if you teach them all, every single one, to your child, what a child you will raise.

America and the world desperately need these teens. Desperately. We are off course, wobbling. In some regards, it looks like we've given up, stopped caring. I know that's not entirely true, but the way we treat some people, my goodness gracious. Breaks my heart. It often seems like the bad guys are winning. If I could put a frowny face here, I'd stack them up in multiple rows.

Let's get to work. Start today and take these 33 strategies to heart. Make them part of your day; mold them to fit your style and personality. Improvise where you need to, and compromise whenever the situation dictates that you should.

Have fun. This is a journey, this raising up of children, an adventure. You got into it because you knew, absolutely knew in the depth of your soul and deep within your heart, it was your destiny. And you were blessed with children—wonderful children perfectly created in God's image! Do you remember the look in their bright baby eyes when they looked to you in anticipation, like *what's next?*!

You're on, Mom and Dad. Start the journey. Explore the uncharted territory of the teenage years. Not with trepidation or fear. But rather, ready for exploration, ready for life in the teen lane, ready for *what's next*!

Author's Note

My wife Nancy and I raised two great kids, a son and a daughter. Don't let anyone tell you that boys aren't any different than girls. When it comes to parenting, they take separate touches, for sure. As I look back on that time when they entered their teen years, I only remember it with fondness. (When I actually wrote that while composing this message, a huge smile spread across my face.) I could tell you stories, and you'd be on the ground laughing. A few stories might make you cry—good tears or reminiscent tears, not sorrowful tears.

Sure, we had a few hiccups. We got one phone call from the police. Not good. Teenage drinking but no arrest, so it turned out to be a learning experience. We got another phone call at two a.m. from college. And again, we all survived, and I bet if we reviewed that second story the next time we are together, we'd get a chuckle out of it. Maybe not a belly laugh, but chuckles are good, too.

All the drama when it happens—if it happens and some did for Nancy and me—seems like a long time ago in a world far, far away. I guess that's my way of saying, you'll survive. But I urge you not to just survive but to grab this opportunity with gusto. The teenage years don't have to be filled with drama and dread!

I began to write about teens in my first novel, *Hard Left*, where I took a fictional look at finding passion early in life and following your dreams. I followed that up with an attempt to write high school curriculum based on the book and sell it to Christian schools in California. Didn't work out that way, but the research and work is now available on my website for free, if you're interested. It's called the *Mentoring Guide*. Although it's structured to work in a small group setting, it can also function quite well as a one-on-one tool for parent and child. It's filled with tips and techniques to build strong teens and teaches lessons about making good choices and decisions in life, building strong relationships, treating others well, expressing yourself, communicating with peers and adults, and learning to deal with bullies and intimidation. The *Mentoring Guide* uses *Hard Left* to illustrate its points, so it's not a stand-alone piece. The book is still in print and often offered at a discount at my website.

Doing my research for this book, I discovered nuances to the way we raised Conor and Kelley. If I had it to do over again—famous last words, huh?—I may have allowed more exploration and dreaming for my son and daughter. Nancy and I weren't overly strict, but I'm sure we could have encouraged them more to explore and take chances in life. They turned out well, and both are very independent and self-reliant, two traits we hold dear and ones that we fostered. They aren't lost twentysomethings trying to figure out what life is all about. If they get stuck, they buckle down and make things happen. They don't come running to Mom and Dad for every little decision in life. That's a good thing because Mom and Dad won't be around forever. My point? There is nothing wrong with freedom in children—freedom to dream, explore, risk, and discover. Con and Kel: if you feel you lost out in those regards, it's never too late! Go on, explore and dream a little more.

I want my readers to know that I am very proud of you both. My son has been successful at the collegiate level in athletics and, as a young adult, as a businessman, a husband,

and a father. My daughter began working when she was sixteen, campaigned aggressively to get into the college of her choice when they put her on a waiting list, is working her way up in business, and has the most infectious personality. Both are exploring anew their relationship with the church and Christ and not following exactly as they were taught as kids. That's good, too. And most of all, they predominately have their mother's great positive attitude about facing life with a smile, a laugh, and knowing that everything will turn out okay. Amen to that!

I consulted many sources for the material of this book. The comedian Steve Harvey and Dr. Phil have both written great books about being successful and raising kids. I thank them for their contributions. I also read and re-read Proverbs from Eugene Peterson's *The Message*. I love the language he uses in that translation of the Bible. It helps my understanding of Biblical truths. Take a look at various Proverbs I highlight below from Peterson's version, and you'll see the correlation to these 33 strategies. Feel free to read Proverbs again, too; there's a cornucopia of wisdom throughout. (Peterson's translation does not numerically label each scripture verse, so I'll list a few examples from different books within Proverbs.)

From Proverbs 11:

When you're kind to others, you help yourself;
when you're cruel to others, you hurt yourself.

The world of the generous gets larger and larger;
the world of the stingy gets smaller and smaller.

The one who blesses others is abundantly blessed;
those who help others are helped.

From Proverbs 12:

Fools have short fuses and explode all too quickly;
the prudent quietly shrug off insults.

Worry weighs us down;
a cheerful word picks us up.

From Proverbs 13:

Refuse discipline and end up homeless;
embrace correction and live an honored life.

Become wise by walking with the wise;
hang out with fools and watch your life fall to pieces.

A refusal to correct is a refusal to love;
love your children by disciplining them.

From Proverbs 16:

Get wisdom—it's worth more than money;
choose insight over income every time.

First pride, then the crash—
the bigger the ego, the harder the fall.

One more thing. I wrote this book with one of the broadest brushes in my toolbox. I know not all parents have the resources to take their children to a zoo or a water park, much less some of the other suggestions I make in the book. Many parents struggle just trying to feed their children and keep them away from trouble. Single parents strain with the daily grind of work and raising kids. I want to offer my encouragement with the advice to not give up, seek help where you can find it, don't be afraid or too prideful to ask for help—and most of all, help each other. Don't become a family living in isolation from one another. We all need each other.

If you ask your Heavenly Father for help, that's always a good step. If you don't know God now, seek ways to find him. A good church, a pastor, or a small Bible study group could help more than you could imagine. The church has its problems in America today, but it's still a place of safety, renewal, and hope. Good luck and God bless.

Santa Barbara, Summer 2021

Resources & Reading List

52 Ways to Connect with Your Smartphone Obsessed Kid, Jonathan McKee. (Shiloh Run Press, 2016)

Don't Sweat the Small Stuff with Your Family, Dr. Richard Carlson. (Hyperion, 1998)

Finding Faith in the Dark, Laurie (Polich) Short. (Zondervan, 2014)

Hard Left (with free *Mentoring Guide)*, Bruce Kirkpatrick. (Lulu Press, 2007)

New Morning Mercies, Paul David Tripp. (Crossway, 2014)

Parenting Today's Adolescent, Dennis & Barbara Rainey, with Bruce Nygren. (Thomas Nelson, 1998)

Parenting with an Attitude: 21 questions successful parent ask themselves, Ed Wimberly. (Christian Faith Publishing, Inc., 2019)

Revolution, George Barna. (Tyndale House Publisher, Inc., 2005)

Right from Wrong: What you need to know to help youth make right choices, Josh McDowell and Bob Hostetler. (Thomas Nelson, 1994)

Seduced, The Grooming of America's Teenagers, Opal Singleton. (Xulon Press, 2015)

Teaching Your Children Healthy Sexuality, Jim Burns. (Bethany House, 2008)

The Happiness Effect: How Social Media is Driving a Generation to Appear Perfect at Any Cost, Donna Freitas. (Oxford University Press, 2017)

The Me I Want to Be, John Ortberg. (Harper Christian Resources, 2014)

The New Tolerance: How a cultural movement threatens to destroy you, your faith, and your children, Josh McDowell and Bob Hostetler. (Tyndale House, 1998)

The Power of a Praying Parent, Stormie Omartian. (Harvest House, 2014)

The Purity Code, Jim Burns. (Bethany House, 2008)

Work with Passion: How to do what you love for a living, Nancy Anderson. (New World Library, 2004)

What Do You Really Want for Your Children?, Dr. Wayne Dyer. (William Morrow and Company, Inc., 1985)

About the Author

Bruce Kirkpatrick writes to inspire people to discover their full measure of God-given gifts and talents. A Pennsylvania boy, he now writes from Southern California. He spent over thirty years in Silicon Valley as an executive and entrepreneur. He now divides his time between writing and serving on nonprofit boards of directors, including Extollo International, a ministry that helps train Haitian men and women in employable skills so that they can find jobs, feed their families, and have hope for the future (Extollo.org). Please visit his website, bkirkpatrick.com.

CPSIA information can be obtained
at www.ICGtesting.com
Printed in the USA
FSHW010349310821
84244FS